MW00973932

The Momager Guide

Empowering Moms to Leave A Loving Legacy

By

Christine M. Martinello

Here's to living + leading with VICTORY!

Love & Light –

Christine Martinello

6-2-12

authorHOUSE

1663 LIBERTY DRIVE, SUITE 200
BLOOMINGTON, INDIANA 47403
(800) 839-8640
www.authorhouse.com

First published by AuthorHouse 09/13/04

ISBN: 1-4184-8178-5 (e)
ISBN: 1-4184-8177-7 (sc)
ISBN: 1-4184-8176-9 (dj)

Printed in the United States of America
Bloomington, Indiana

This book is printed on acid-free paper.

Dedication

This book is dedicated to the Creator.
I wrote it for Moms who represent
God's creative and nurturing force in the world today.
I hope women will know their power and
speak boldly with a united voice of love.
The greatest force on earth always has been
And always will be Love.
This book is also dedicated to my amazing
husband Bob, and children David, Tina Rose, and Steven.
Thanks for teaching me how
To unconditionally love.

Dearest Mommy

By Bob, David, Tina, and Steven Martinello

Mothers are a special breed.
They spend all day with "I NEED" "I NEED."
In each act every child makes,
Mom has to overlook lots of mistakes.
Her loving gaze coaxes and encourages smiles
Through all the tantrums and the trials.

Mom, your job has special rewards.
Today, we give you this grand award.
Not money, fame or a brand new car,
But a love note from the cookie jar.
There is no higher calling than to give yourself away
To the cause of loving us each and every day.

We love you more than life itself
Which you gave us from your very self.
And we give you back this heartfelt praise,
MOM YOU'RE THE BEST – HIP HIP HOORAYS!!!

Just in case that is still not enough,
MOM WE LOVE YOU, and you're "HOT STUFF."

Acknowledgments

Giving birth to this book has been similar to the journey of bringing a child into the world. I've been blessed because every step of the way people have shared their ideas, gifts, and wisdom.

My heartfelt thanks and a deep sense of gratitude to all who joined me on this journey:

- To God, for giving me direction, wisdom, and continual strength. He is the co-author.

- To Bob, my dear husband, who believes in me, sometimes more than I believe in myself. Thanks for encouraging me and being my partner in parenting and life.

- To David, Tina Rose, and Steven. You're awesome children! Thanks for giving me the privilege of leading. You've taught me and continue to teach me the meaning of unconditional love.

- To my family and friends. Especially my Mama and Dad, brother Joe and sister Joy. Wendy McDonough, Kathy Winter, Erika Vendrella, Eunice Giaquinto, and countless other friends. (You know who you are!) Thanks for listening to an endless stream of ideas and supporting me every baby step of the way.

- To Jennifer Beavers, my writing partner, for her constant interest, and purity of soul.

- To Toni Robino. She was more than an editor, she was a midwife.

- To the University of Dayton Women's Center and Literary Committee for your invaluable feedback.

- To my Marketing Mamas for your overflowing enthusiasm to share these messages.

- To Moms who shared their stories.

- To Moms who feed souls and nurture with an open heart.

CONTENTS

Introduction

MOMAGERS© rule!

Why am I writing this book and how can it empower you?

Deep within me, I realize this book is a combination of my life's passion and work up to this point. Lucky for you - you get to take advantage of all the lessons I've learned and mistakes I've made. Believe me, there's been plenty of both! My hope is that you will draw new ideas and wisdom from some of the world's greatest leaders -- to strengthen yourself as a leader and to strengthen your family.

Perhaps you're wondering if Moms really do have leadership skills and if so, what could they be?

Carol Bellamy, Executive Director of the United Nation's Children Fund explains "Leadership isn't just for leaders. Ensuring the rights and well being of children is the key to sustained development in every country and to peace and security in the world. Meeting this responsibility fully, consistently, and at any cost, is the essence of leadership."

To change our culture and businesses, and to strengthen our families, we all need to be leaders.

Life is complicated. I know how hard it can be living in our turbulent and hectic world. Sometimes I long to live in the stories my grandmother used to tell me about how simple life was when she was a girl. Yet, we all know we can't go back.

To move powerfully forward into our future and to lay the groundwork for our children and their children, we need incredible courage, strength, and moral conviction. Applying the seven VICTORY© leadership skills contained in this book will bring about positive changes in your life and in your family for generations to come. Learning how to be a MOMAGER is a set of refined and complex skills you can possess to influence those around you. This knowledge can bring about revolutionary changes in your life, helping you to lead the life you want. As we all know, "knowledge is power."

As a leadership trainer, I knew the leadership skills that applied at work and I slowly discovered they transferred to the home. Many years ago, (too many to mention now), my husband Bob and I started discussing what type of family life we wanted. Having three children in three and a half years didn't leave us much planning time early on, but eventually (once the sleep deprivation coma lifted) we started applying some leadership principles to our home life. Guess what topic we started with? Conflict resolution! We had two toddlers running around the house and conflict was running rampant. And guess what else? It worked! Before our very eyes our home-life started becoming more peaceful and less hurried. Our family focused on solving problems instead of complaining and criticizing. Ahhhh, there's hope.

Then we moved into team building and communication skills. Before I knew it, the yelling mom (who I never liked anyway) disappeared, only to be replaced by the confident, fun mom. Imagine that! After a few years we tried all the leadership principles, and our family life has changed dramatically for the better. In the meantime, we realized that consistently applying all these leadership principles was helping us strengthen our leadership abilities in the office.

A recent study by the Center for Research on Women at Wellesley College found that parenting skills transfer to the work world. Sixty female leaders, including politicians, CEO's and media and TV, revealed that they used maternal and family roles to describe their leadership abilities. Mothering was the metaphor that defined their leadership

Anne Altman is a just one example of the many executives who have discovered their leadership skills transfer between work and home. Anne is an IBM executive who accepted a one-year assignment in New York, away from her husband and kids. "Without one of us stepping back to focus on the kids, we knew we'd miss too much," she said. During that assignment, Anne learned many lessons about balancing and delegating. Her husband took over the day-to-day duties and decided to work part-time. She went home on the weekends and threw every ounce of time and energy into her family.

She took up horseback riding with her daughter and volunteered to teach Sunday school at the family's church.

As time passed, she discovered a balance that had escaped her for years. Before taking the job in New York, "even when I was at home, I wasn't engaged," she said. "I would never just sit down and play with the kids."

It wasn't easy for Anne to share control over family matters with her husband. She explained, "While I was in New York, I still tried to take ownership. I'd ask my husband: "What did you get? Was it appropriate?" She learned to let go, allowing her husband to get more involved. "It's like delegating at work -- giving others responsibility, knowing that what ever they do, it's for the team as a whole. But I was much better at learning that in the work world."

The irony is that many of us know that leadership principles work well in the office, but not everyone realizes how well they apply to our home-lives. There is still a "disconnect" between the two worlds. I was raised to believe that work was much more important and challenging than being a "housewife." Early on in my career, I felt I had to prove my worth to myself and the world by making plenty of money and having a successful career. Boy, was I wrong. Success can be found in many arenas and work is only one of them.

I believe the most important and longest-lasting contribution we will make is in the family. That's why I've created new terms and ideas to describe the challenges we face. These concepts will prepare you to be the best woman, mom, wife, sister, aunt and grandmother, leader and manager that you can be.

The leadership skills I'll share with you are based on "generational-centered leadership"™. This type of leadership cares about making long-term, positive impact in the family and in the world.

One of the first steps to take is to add the term MOMAGER to your vocabulary, mom and manager mixed into one. This new term redefines the challenging role mom's really have. I cherish being a mom and am extremely proud of my role as mother. I have to admit, I used to be a bit embarrassed when someone at a cocktail party asked, "What do you do?" and I replied, "I'm a mom." Nine times out of ten, that was the beginning of the end of the conversation. This book will educate women and men alike about the real leadership skills Momagers™ have. Today, when someone asks me what I do, I say, "I'm a Momager!" That simple statement, spoken with pride, has proven to make conversations much more interesting!

When I'm facilitating leadership development seminars, most of the participants are men in management and leadership at the manager, director and vice-president levels. As my son David says: "Mom, you teach some really important people. They really listen to you?" Kids teach us so much about being humble. What has pained me is the absence of women in the training. Sure, there are some women, but not enough. I've been very fortunate to learn from and teach wonderful leaders. Not all ladies are so lucky. Now, you will be! This book is written for you to learn "best-practices" from great leaders.

The Momager Guide is my gift to you. My sincere hope is that this book will help to bring women together and uplift us in our journey. As you begin reading Chapter One, ponder the question, "What legacy do I want to leave behind?" By the end of the book, you will be able to answer that question with much greater certainty and you'll have the skills and tools to make it happen.

Enjoy the journey.

Chapter 1

"What is a Momager and How Does She Lead?"

*"Being a mother, as far as I can tell, is a constantly evolving
process of adapting to the needs of your child while also
changing and growing as a person in your own right."*
- Deborah Insel, Founder, Helping Teens Succeed

Leadership is important in all areas of life, but leading as a mom is essential. I had my own epiphany about this one cold November morning that I will always remember. As my five-year-old daughter, Tina Rose and I left our cozy, warm home and ventured out into the cold, dark morning, we noticed the stars shining brightly, and the icy air took our breath away.

We were walking, hand-in-hand to my daughter's bus stop, looking up at the bright stars and feeling the comfortable silence of being together.

My daughter looked up at me and asked, "Mommy, do I go to daycare after school today?"

"No honey, today I will be home after school and we'll spend the rest of the day together," I responded.

Tina jumped up and down and yelled. "Hip Hip Hooray, today's a Mommy Care© day!"

Of all the people in the entire world, my daughter wanted *me* to guide her. As the bus drove away, I walked back home with tears freezing on my cheeks and eyelashes. A range of emotions washed over me. I felt joyful that she was so happy we spend days together. (Perhaps she forgot the yelling mom). I felt sadness that these times were passing so very quickly and I wished I could stop time – if only for a while. (How many times before, had I thought, when are they going to grow up?!) I felt guilt that perhaps she was spending too much time in day care and away from me. (How can two days a week be too much? Especially after I spent years sacrificing financially and professionally to work only two days each week.) Am I doing enough as a mom? What am I doing as a mom? As mothers, we have the dubious distinction of being able to feel dozens of conflicting emotions simultaneously.

My discovery was more brilliant than the brightest star in that black predawn sky. I AM A MOM *AND* I AM A LEADER! That day, I wanted to shout it from the rooftop. (As if the neighbors need another thing to chat about.) The realization touched my core and shook me awake to a new reality. Leadership wasn't reserved to my work outside the home. Leadership wasn't solely the domain of men in business and government. What could possibly be more important than leading today's children – tomorrow's leaders?

That day I began to form a new understanding and appreciation of a woman's career as a mom. Today, my career is as a leader and mom, a MOMAGER. And, thanks to my daughter, the term Mommy Care© days was born. Mommy Care© days are the precious days that moms and children spend together. Mommy Care© days are the days when Mom is the leader! And so, the journey began for me to be a mom who leads her family instead of following.

Motherhood has bittersweet moments. Leadership does too. I was determined to become a leader in my home. The problem was, I didn't have anywhere to go to learn how to do this. My mother was not a career woman, and other women I talked to all seemed to be "surviving" or "juggling" but did not seem content and satisfied. They didn't seem to be having fun or enjoying life. I had no role models. I couldn't relate to the leaders I saw on TV. They all seemed so put together and perfect. I realized something different needed to be created to achieve success in this new marketplace. The difference was a change in perspective regarding the deepening value of what women really do in all areas of their lives.

Learning how to become a Momager will provide you the opportunity to change both your present situation and your future in positive and powerful ways. Being a mom has empowered my life and taught me how to be a strong leader.

You are about to begin a journey of discovery into a world of leadership. A path that only leaders with courage, guts, and diaper changing experience should walk down. (Let's talk about real strength, okay?) This journey will lead you to recreate your life according to your own rules and values.

So, let's talk. Make a cup of tea, or coffee, find your most comfortable spot and snuggle up. Imagine some of the world's most influential moms are with you to mentor, support, and help you on your journey. (And you don't even have to "dress for success" or bother doing your hair or make-up.) This is your own private, personal, growth time. All the secrets to successful mothering and leadership will be shared.

What's a MOMAGER?

Not "Just a Mom" Anymore

*"The commonest fallacy among women is that simply
having children makes one a mother - which is as absurd as believing that
having a piano makes one a musician."*
-Sydney J. Harris, *The Authentic Person and Winners and Losers*

A Momager is a new blend of woman. She is a mom and manager united into one powerful package. She makes family her number one priority and has strong leadership abilities, which she applies, in many areas of life. She can be a "stay-at-home" mom or a "working mom." Although I don't like either of those terms, until Momager, there were no other terms that truly define what mothers do. "The term 'working mother' is redundant," says Jane Sellman, in *Humanity/Parenthood*. Speaking for myself, when I was a "stay-at-home" mom, I wasn't really staying at home much. A Momager can move in and out of the workplace and apply her skills in the world of motherhood and the world of business.

I believe that each of us has been put on this earth for a reason and it's our job to fulfill our destiny. Some of us do. Some of us don't even know where to begin. If you've been blessed to be a mother, your destiny is one of the highest callings of leadership and self-sacrifice. It is also a journey of incredible growth. To be effective, you must accept the challenges, joys, and power you need to be successful as a mom and manager united, a MOMAGER.

Make no mistake about it, we have been sold a lie. Society would have us believe that anyone who makes money is of value and the more money you make the more valuable you are. Think about it. If you work outside the home you get paid. So when asked, "What do you do?" Most people immediately spout their job title.

Think about the job of motherhood. You could hire someone to do everything a mother does and spend a fortune fast. Add all this up. How much does it cost to replace mom? How expensive is a CEO, good nanny, psychiatrist, decorator, home organizer, cleaning woman, chef, and chauffeur?

Just for fun (and shock value) let's estimate what an average mom of three children might be worth, knowing full well that there is really no way to put a dollar figure on our services. Ann Crittenden, author of *The Price of Motherhood*, calls the best test for valuing unpaid labor the "third person criterion." If a third person could be paid to do the activity, then it is work. Cooking, cleaning, childcare and yard work, for example, all fall into that category.

Service	Frequency	Average Market Rate	Annual Expense
Childcare	50 hours/week	9.00/hour	$23,400
Housekeeper	2 cleanings/ week	$60.00/ cleaning	$ 6,240
Chef/Grocery Shopping/ Dietician	20 hours/week	$20.00/hour	$20,800
Financial Manager	2 hours/week	$75.00/hour	$ 7,800
Chauffer	11 round trips/ wk-events, doctor visits, etc.	$12.00/trip	$ 6,864
Laundry	6 hours/week	$20.00/hour	$ 3,120
Psychologist	5 hours/week	$125/hour	$32,500
Personal Shopper	2 hours/week	$30.00/hour	$ 3,120
Management Expert	6 hours/week	$125.00/ hour	$39,000
TOTAL			$142,844 *

*Based on Midwestern prices

And that doesn't even include everything Moms do. Think about the things you do and add them to your base salary. Here are some other duties Mom's do that should be considered.

- Decorator
- Teacher and/or Home Schooler
- Nurse -- day and night duty -- My husband offered me $150 if I woke up with the baby one night when we were both exhausted. I wouldn't take it because sleep was more important that night.
- Spiritual Guide
- Gardener
- Activities Director-Party/event planner
- Animal caretaker
- Photographer/Scrapbooker/Family Historian
- Massage Therapist
- Official Family Nurturer -- they always yell, "MOM"
- Seamstress
- Caring for an elderly/sick parent
- Librarian
- Home organizer

Wrapping all this into one woman is, well,.........*priceless.*

"No one's crazy enough to work for free but moms," says Ric Edelman, whose firm, Edelman Financial Services estimates a mom's worth is estimated at $508,700 per year. "And no one has enough money to hire a good mom . . . From that perspective our mothers are indeed priceless."

We live in challenging, fast-paced times. We live in the era of the global marketplace, where every day the ebb and flow of supply and demand determines economic direction. Our lives are hectic and information overload is ongoing. Change is constant. More new information has been produced in the last 30 years than in the previous 500 years. Can you believe that?

Let's take a good look at what is happening in the world today. Our headlines are filled with devastating news of war, accounting fraud, teenage pregnancies, white collar crime, company losses that wipe out retirement dreams, unprecedented violence and disrespect in our schools, high divorce rates and a weakening family structure.

The government has passed the Corporate Reform Bill to try to curb corporate scandals. Millions of dollars are invested in abstinence training for our teens. While the government can legislate business and social ethics, we cannot legislate our way to integrity. The responsibility for doing what is right always has been and always will be the individual's responsibility. That means you and me, doing what is right and leading others to do the same.

We each have to develop strong character and instill those values in our children. Why? Quite simply, our future depends on it. This world could use a little shaping up don't you think? Our children and our children's children are depending on us.

Now, more than ever, we need women of strong moral conviction and character. Being a MOMAGER is being a woman who leads and builds strong families, businesses, and communities. Momagers leave a loving legacy.

My hope is that you will draw new ideas and wisdom from some of the world's greatest leaders -- to strengthen yourself as a leader and to strengthen your family, organizations, and communities. Of course, this can lead to personal and professional growth. I firmly believe you have the power within you to determine your success. This book will provide a framework and the tools to become a wonderful leader. (If you're already a strong leader, Momager principles will help you to become even stronger.) This book is my gift to you so you can be educated and empowered in leadership.

Why Do Women Need to be Leaders?

Look around and you'll see plenty of men in the highest-ranking leadership positions and the occasional woman. Mostly men are in government positions. Mostly men are in the top corporate and non-profit organization boards. For years, mostly men have attended my training programs for leadership development.

When I *do* have the occasional woman in my session, they immediately come up to me during a break or lunch. We have a common bond. It's like they need to refill their water canteens after walking miles in the desert. We quench each other's thirst for knowledge. They always have this question: How can I be a woman *and* a leader? For the most part, only other women can understand our unique situation.

It is estimated we will each influence more than 10,000 people during our lifetime. Isn't that amazing? So, the question is not *if* you will influence others, but *how* you will influence them? Will you use your influence for short-term gain or to establish a long-term legacy? The choice is yours. What will you do? How will you lead?

For women to move forward we need to redefine what it means to be a woman today and in the future. This book will support you in growing your own new definitions. In America, there's social and legal support for women. However, there's no framework for women to take the step into power.

Every woman is faced with challenging questions, such as, "How can I be feminine and powerful?" and "Who's going to change society and our workplaces to embrace a woman's uniqueness and contributions in the world?" The answers? We are.

We can do this by becoming leading ladies equipped with the seven VICTORY leadership skills©. This leadership style encompasses what women have done for many years and is becoming highly valuable in the new work environment -- Leading by serving others.

"A common theme present in most discussions of leadership for the 21st century is the leader's ability to create, articulate, and communicate, not only a vision, but, more importantly, a global vision." These words by Karin Klenke, author of *Women and Leadership* highlight what's important for us in order to move forward. If we want to survive and thrive in these challenging times, leading is a necessity.

Perhaps you're wondering if women and moms really have leadership skills, and if so, what are they? Because, after all, our society doesn't equate motherhood with leadership. We tend to think of leaders as CEOs, presidents, great spiritual people, media celebrities, and high-ranking government officials. We think of people like Mother Theresa, Rudy Giuliani, and Martin Luther King;

people who have thousands of people following them. It's true that these are examples of great leaders, however, we are all leaders of our own lives. If we are mothers, we are whisked into a leadership position by leading our families. (Whether we like it or not.)

Madeline Metzger, a development professional at the University of Dayton, Ohio, mother of three, and grandmother of seven, shares this story about her realization of the impact she has on her family.

"I remember a time, a couple of years ago, when my adult daughter made a comment. She said, 'Mom, don't you realize you're the matriarch of the family? Don't you realize how the whole family looks up to you and follows your lead?' 'They do?' I replied. And I thought, 'Oh shoot! Now I have to do everything right.' I wondered, 'Hey, if I'm such a leader, how come you didn't take my advice?' My son and daughter-in-law were looking to us (my husband and I) for advice on their teenager and I was thinking 'Why are you asking me? Do you think we had the perfect score here?' But, it's obvious they look to us for guidance, and I was just standing there praying that I was going to say the right words to my children who are concerned for their children." The legacy of influence passes from one generation to the next.

The bad news is, it takes time to develop leadership skills. The good news is that the Momager Guide can significantly shorten your learning curve. There's hope and it's a great time to reap the benefits of leading effectively. At this time in history, women have more clout and opportunities than we have had for thousands of years. Being a Momager will allow you to reap many rewards from being a more valuable and productive employee to having more harmony and control over your home life.

Don't confuse a Momager with a Super Mom.

A Momager is a Mom who's real about mothering and strives to do her best by loving her children and family. A Super Mom is a woman who tries to accomplish everything and sets up the illusion of "doing it all."

Confessions of a Momager

I admit to:

Sending them to school with store bought cookies, disguised as homemade cookies.

Yelling at my kids

Giving up yelling at my kids for lent.

Apologizing for the mistakes I've made.

Learning from every experience.

Wanting to escape the responsibility and never-ending pressure as a Mom.

Spanking my kids.

Not having all the answers.

Yet, I know I can reach out to other Moms and ask their advice.

I can trust my instincts and intuition to do the right thing for my children.

I can be honest about the trials and triumphs of mothering.

And I know that I am proud I am a Mom!

A Momager is present, loving, real.

What is Leadership?

Let's clearly understand what leadership means. Here's what some experts have to say:

Laurie Beth Jones, author of *Jesus CEO: Using Ancient Wisdom for Visionary Leadership*:

Leaders identify, articulate, and summarize concepts that motivate others. Most important, they boil concepts down to an understandable idea.

Margaret Thatcher, former Prime Minister of England: I cannot manage the past. There are other people in my government who manage the present. It is my unique responsibility as the leader to shine a spotlight on the future, and marshal the support of my own countrymen to create that future.

Peter Drucker, Management guru for the past 60 years:

Leadership involves attracting and keeping followers.

John Maxwell, Author of many leadership books including *The 21 Irrefutable Laws of Leadership*: Leadership is about influencing others. Real leadership is being the person others will gladly and confidently follow.

David Martinello, a wise child (age 4): A leader is a person who's in-charge. People look to the leader for the way to go.

All of these definitions contain two common threads. First, a leader must have followers that gladly and confidently follow them. Think of the way ducklings follow their mother duck. If you believe you're a leader but don't have people who follow you, think again. There's a big difference between being in a leadership position and being a true leader. So take a look behind you once in a while and make sure they're still following you.

The second common thread is that leaders take action to accomplish their vision or their group's vision. Based on these commonalties, my definition of a leader is a person who influences others to follow and leaves a lasting legacy.

There are "real leaders" who do it right and practice the principles contained in this book. Then there are "pretend leaders." These are people who have been promoted to a leadership position but don't really know how to lead. Our goal as Momagers is to be real leaders who make life-long positive impacts.

As I was embarking on my new path as a Momager, I had the pleasure of witnessing my son David in a leadership role.

In the pre-school hallway, nine children, all in single file, were walking toward me led by David. He was proudly walking in the front of the line holding the "leadership stick" high in the air. The stick was a three-foot broomstick with a red "flip-flop" attached at the top. Initially, I couldn't help but laugh. But, seeing the look of seriousness and determination on David's face quickly changed my look to one of importance and pride. He briefly glanced at me and continued walking with his head held high. He was leading his fellow students into the classroom. "I had important leadership work to do," he later told me.

When David and I talked about leadership, here's what he said: "A leader is the person who's in charge and people look at the leader for the way to go. A leader helps us know where to go (so we don't get lost) and everyone follows the leader. Everyone should get a turn being the leader so they know what it's like. I sure had fun holding the leader stick!"

Well, can you imagine how humble I felt? There I was, a corporate trainer teaching "leadership development," and my 4-year-old son crystallized the definition of leadership more clearly than I had! (Wow - he learns fast. Of course he does, he's my son.) Children have such wisdom! And, they teach us how to lead every day. We must be open to learning.

Women are incredibly powerful leaders. When given the opportunity and environment, women thrive. Look around you. Women are leading in more and more ways every day, and in every way. Sisters, we have traded in the aprons for astronaut helmets. Now there are women doctors, CEO's, inventors, police officers, engineers, navy and army officers, and senators. In these competitive times, women are rising to the top of many professions that were earlier reserved "for men only." After 200 years of the women's rights movement, the world has reached a place where women are finally getting the recognition we deserve in the professional arena.

The Fight to Become Leaders

Let's take a brief look back in history to see how far we've come. In the 1800's, women were considered second-class citizens. Unfortunately, in 75 percent of the world, women are still treated as secondary to men. Women were labeled as the weaker sex, both physically and mentally. Girls were only allowed to attend schools for boys when there was room. Usually, girls learned to read and write in separate schools called dame schools, run by women teachers in their homes. When a woman married, she gave up any and all rights she had. Laws didn't allow women to vote, own property, divorce, or have custody of their own children. If women "had to work," they were limited to working in factories, as housekeepers, governesses, and rarely as writers or teachers.

It wasn't until Aug. 18, 1920, seventy-two years after the first women's rights convention, that women in the United States won the right to vote. With the passage of the Equal Rights Amendment in 1972, we saw a flood of women entering the workforce and college.

Today, women have access to all professions. We have words like "sexual harassment" and "battered women," and we have laws protecting women from abuse. We have maternity leave and paternity leave, so families can be together and welcome our little ones into the world. We have networks of women mentoring and helping each other. We have come so far and we are fortunate to have so many opportunities. We can learn much from our past and applaud the brave women who have brought us to this point in history. Now we have so many more choices to make.

We are on a continuum of growth. We have a long legacy of powerful women behind us. Still, we have a long way to go. We still have sexual harassment and women are still being victimized at alarming rates. We have paternity leave but most families can't afford this unpaid absence from work, especially right after they have a baby.

We don't have peace in many of our families. We don't have a critical mass of women in politics to change many of the issues affecting women. Millions of women and children are in poverty. Oh yes, we have a long way to go.

What have we lost in the past 50 years? As women, we have lost our way in cherishing and respecting our role as creators and sustainers of life. We have been so busy building careers outside the home that we have discounted and even ignored our role inside the home as mothers. Home-economics classes have been replaced with computer classes. Our children are in crisis. There is a moral decay amongst leaders. We've lost an understanding that each individual is of unique value. We have lost deep roots, connection to family and friends, and perhaps, worst of all, we have lost a feeling of meaning in our lives. Maybe we threw out the baby with the bath water. Is it time we brought the baby back in?

We stand on the brink of a new world that demands incredible courage, strength, and moral conviction to move forward. We realize our careers and home life are not just about amassing more and more money. (Although that would be nice too, wouldn't it?) Our lives are about something deeper. They are about leadership -- having our say in our own unique way. Making things happen. Instilling our beliefs in the future. Where we choose to apply our leadership skills is up to each of us individually, but we all have vital roles to play as leaders.

It is time to be powerful leading ladies with loving hearts and strong minds. It is time to find our full potential in all arenas of life. It is time to re-define and re-invent womanhood. It is time to move forward with dignity and strength and true equal opportunities. How do we do this? By recognizing our potential and rising to the challenges before us.

As women, it means lifting each other up, instead of comparing whose contribution is the greatest. Have you noticed the competition among mothers and families? Who has the first child to walk? What college is Junior going to? How much TV time do you allow your kids? Do your kids do chores? Motherhood is not a competitive sport! Each mother develops in her own unique timing and way and so does each child.

Moving forward means recognizing all our strengths and celebrating women's accomplishments in the workplace, community, and home. Uplifting, positive contributions build a stronger society for everyone. You know there are two ways to have the tallest building in town. One is to build it. The second way is to knock down all the other buildings. Which way are you going to grow to your greatest height?

Mothers "In-charge" as Leaders

Momagers are some of the most influential leaders! The influence of our mothers' on our character is one that molds us for the rest of our lives. A mother has long-term, widespread impact on her children, business, society, and the world. During the Outstanding Business Leaders Award Ceremony, Linnett Daily, CEO of 1st Interstate Bank of Texas said, "The influence of our mothers on our character -- and the influence of character on our business success -- has been extraordinarily impactful."

However, there is trouble in paradise. As women, we still don't recognize our uniqueness in all areas of our lives. The boom of women entering and exiting the workforce over the last 40 years has created a new generation of women. The conflict exists. Women are being torn in so many different directions and we see the ripple effects. With all this progress, we still have some questions to explore, and some serious issues to solve.

- Why is a woman in America beaten by her husband or partner every 15 seconds (on average)?
- Why is the divorce rate over 50 percent?
- Why do we have such conflict about what is "fair" within our marriages?
- Why do we have a lack of women leaders to represent us in government? (Women represent only about 14 percent of the U.S. Congress and House of Representatives.)
- Why is depression on the increase for women and children?
- Why does America have the highest teen suicide rate?
- What are we going to do about all the women trapped in poverty and on the margins of society?
- Why are millions of children and mothers without health insurance?
- What are we going to do about our children's obesity problem?
- Why are so few (if any) women happy with their bodies? (75 percent of college women don't feel good about their bodies and 45 percent of today's nine-year old girls are dieting.)
- Why do 8 million women suffer from anorexia and bulimia?
- Why do we still fear negotiating for a fair and competitive salary?

These are some serious problems we have to wrestle with. We can hear these alarming facts and see we have challenges ahead of us. Who is going to try and solve all these problems? We are. We have unlimited opportunities and are at a unique point in history to express our voices. Fortunately, we have both major influence and financial power and they are growing each day.

- One in every 10 adult women is a business owner.
- Women businesses employ 18.2 million people and generate 2.3 trillion dollars in annual sales.
- Women control 80 percent of household spending.

Let's admit how tough it really is to be a successful woman these days. So, while "we've come a long way baby," we still have a long way to go. But, before you begin to think it's all hopeless, read on.

Ladies, we have a tremendous amount of choice as to how we'll invest our time and energy. Women know what it's like to gain satisfaction and intellectual stimulation from interesting careers. We also know we have a limited amount of time to raise a family and we want to leave a lasting legacy. Making wise choices and feeling confident in these decisions can be difficult and agonizing at times.

What can women do? Should we invest heavily in careers only to find emptiness and regret in our home lives? Should we stay at home to raise children and sacrifice growing in new skills and abilities? Should we work part-time, flex-time, and other variations of work schedules so we can balance both work and home? Should we "sequence" our career and forego employment for a season of life to nurture our family? The options can make women feel like they have vertigo! Each woman is faced with myriad choices. No matter what a woman decides, she typically discovers that she needs to adopt a fresh reality by acquiring new skills and approaches to be successful. By becoming a strong leader you can meet all the challenges with wisdom and long-term vision.

In order to meet these challenges, a shift in understanding and a deeper application of leadership skills is needed. In this new environment, many of the skills used to keep harmony in the home are the same ones used with peers in the office.

In America, a mini-migration is taking place. According to a recent article in *Business Week* magazine, many female professionals at the very peak of their careers are quitting to stay home with their kids. More mothers are making kids their career of choice. An article in *USA Today* highlighted that in the year 2000, women working with children under one year old has dropped for the first time in nearly 25 years. Women working dropped from nearly 60 percent in 1998 to 55 percent in 2000.

According to a *Time* magazine article, ("The Case for Staying Home," March 22, 2004) for dual-career couples with kids under 18, the combined work hours have grown from 81 a week in 1977 to 91 in 2002 according the Families and Work Institute. We are now the workaholism capital of the world, surpassing the Japanese, laments sociologist Arlie Hochschild, author of *The Time Bind: When Work Becomes Home and Home Becomes Work.*

Meanwhile, the pace has quickened on the home front, where a mother's job has expanded to include managing a packed schedule of child-enhancement activities. Nowadays, the article says, our culture insists that "to be a remotely decent mother, a woman has to devote her entire physical, psychological, emotional, and intellectual being, 24/7, to her children." It's a standard that's impossible to meet. But that sure doesn't stop women from trying.

Census data reveal an uptick in stay-at-home moms who hold graduate or professional degrees -- the very women who seemed destined to blast through the glass ceiling. Now 22 percent of them are home with their kids. A study by Catalyst found that one in three women with MBAs are not working fulltime (It's one in twenty for their male peers).

"Younger women have greater expectations about the work-life balance," says Joanne Brundage, 51, founder and Executive Director of Mothers & More, a mothers' support organization with 7,500 members and 180 chapters in the U. S.

While boomer moms have been reluctant to talk about their children at work for fear the "people won't think you're a professional," she observes, younger women feel more entitled to ask for changes and advocate for themselves."

Reach Advisors found that 51 percent of Gen X moms were home full time, compared with 33 percent of boomer moms. Hunter College Sociologist Pamela Stone says, "Many of the women I talked to have tried to work part time or put forth job-sharing plans, and they're shot down. Despite all the family friendly rhetoric, the workplace for professionals is extremely, extremely inflexible."

Pam Pala, 35, hopes to return to work when her daughter is in school, and she desperately hopes she won't be penalized for her years at home. "I have a feeling that I'll have to start lower on the totem pole than where I left," she says. "It seems unfair."

Will corporate culture evolve to a point where employees feel genuinely encouraged to use flexible work options? On-ramps, slow lanes, flexible options and respect for all such pathways can't come soon enough for mothers who are eager to set examples and offer choices for the next generation.

Michael Elliott writes, "The incessant demands of an always-on 24/7 world of free information have made some middle-aged women who'd like to go back to work consider whether the benefits are worth the hassle. But so long as they stay out of the labor market, their husbands are trapped in it -- otherwise family incomes would fall. Hence that familiar social phenomenon: a married couple in their 50's in which the wife is resentful because she does too little paid work and the husband is resentful because he does too much. Thirty years ago, we dreamed of something different. Pity it didn't work out."

Terry Laughlin, 38, a stay-at-home mom and former psychology professor says, "I want to make sure my girls realize that although it's wonderful staying at home, that's only one of many options. What I hope to show them is that at some point I can re-create myself and go back to work."

Women like Brenda Barnes, President and CEO of Pepsi North America, are choosing to be leaders in their homes. In 1997, at 43, Barnes decided to leave her career, despite her success. "After years of hectic travel, dinner meetings, missing children's birthdays and even living in separate cities from her husband, Barnes decided to go home full time. She said, "Now I need to give my family more of my time."

Millions of women are deciding that the most family-friendly career option is "sequencing" -- foregoing employment for a season of life to nurture a family. "You have to make your choices -- maybe I burned at both ends for too long," said Barnes.

Women choosing to stay home are discovering three things.

1. Mothering is a lot harder than we thought.
2. Stay-at-home motherhood is the perfect training ground for leadership.
3. We need to value the time we have in motherhood and recognize the amazing contribution we're making as MOMAGERS.

Women want to grow and unleash their full potential in every area of their lives. Living a life similar to our mothers and grandmothers does not bring contentment. We are charting a new course and like the early pioneer women, we stand alone to discover how to best handle each situation.

The world is changing rapidly and our roles have changed dramatically. According to *USA Today*, the five greatest concerns parents and teachers had about children in the 1950's were: talking out of turn, chewing gum in class, doing homework, stepping out of line, and cleaning their rooms. The top five concerns today are: drug addiction, teen pregnancy, suicide and homicide, gang violence, and anorexia/bulimia. We have new challenges and new realities. Women are called upon to lead at new levels of responsibility, compete with men, and mother within a new social environment.

If you could do it all again, what would you do differently?

In 1994, I was a guest speaker at an Executive Women International conference at the prestigious Park Lane Hotel in London, England. I was going to speak to some of the best and brightest women leaders in the world and I was really excited. We were discussing global communications and the impact of globalization on business. The press was there. Forty million people would watch us on TV. I felt on top of the world and the power felt great! This was the big league! People listened to me and I was leading women in their ideas and views.

After the presentation, we had a panel discussion. A woman from the audience asked, "What would you do differently if you had your life to live over again?" (Don't you just love those simple questions?)

I will never forget what Lynne Franks, the owner of the third largest public relations firm in England and an adviser to the United Nations, said.

"I have had everything in life. I have all the money I would want. I have a wonderful family. I have great clothes. I have a good enough figure and I am healthy. However, one thing I would do differently is I would have spent more time with my children, especially when they were young. You see, I was so busy with my career that I really didn't give my children what they needed. Achieving balance between work and home would be what I would do differently."

A smart, successful woman who had everything simply wished she could turn back time and spend more time with her children!

At that moment, I fought back tears. You see, I had a secret. My first child, my newborn son David, was at home. Deep down I believed I could work, build my career, and be a great mom. I believed I could "do it all" and be happy. I honestly thought, "This child isn't really going to change my life." I was in my early 30's and at a pinnacle point in my career. Was I really going to give up my career to spend more time with this tiny gurgling baby?

I had an instant "wake-up call." The hard questions in life came tumbling around me. What were my priorities? How much time was I willing to invest in my family, career, and children? Those questions haunted and challenged me for a long time. They will haunt you too until you answer them honestly based on your own values.

The decisions I had to make involved re-creating myself. At that time, my baby and my role as mom was more important than working outside the home. I chose to make family my first priority, and my role as mother my career. (My friend Leigh Ann said 'the mommy gene finally kicked in.') I realized that the days are fleeting and I could never get the time back later, after my children were grown.

I chose to be a mother who leads her family. That choice has altered my life forever. If you are a mother or considering being a mother, I encourage you to clearly consider your priorities and focus your time and resources accordingly. Your choice will be uniquely fitted to your situation and may change many times before you get it just right. Flexibility is key, especially since you and your family will be continually changing and growing.

For years, I struggled with the loss of power in my career and my growth in the role of mom. And many more years later, I found myself struggling with the reverse -- the loss of influence as a parent and growth in my career. As women, we need never-ending flexibility from our workplaces and we are the ones to lobby for it -- just one step at a time, with our boss and co-workers.

How Does Leadership Apply to Motherhood?

What do mother's really do? (We know they don't eat bon bons all day, right?) Mothers raise children. What does that mean? A mom's job is to lead and influence the next generation of leaders. Mothers influence their children whether they are great or deficient mothers. Having a baby doesn't make you a good mother. It takes time to learn how to lead well at home.

There is no question that a mom is a leader. She is in a leadership position by being a mom. The question is, "How is Mom going to lead? Is she going to be a hierarchical dictator? Maybe for a day or so, but then she discovers, it doesn't work effectively. (NO is a toddler's favorite word). Is she going to be a soft leader and let her kids do whatever they want? Is she going to let them make family decisions based on their wants? Or is she going to be an effective mom and use the same skills any successful leader uses to influence and motivate people? I believe motherhood is the best training ground for leadership because each woman learns how to lead "on the job."

A recent study by the Center for Research on Women at Wellesley College found that skills needed for motherhood transfer to the work world. Sixty female leaders, including politicians, CEOs, celebrities, and media personalities, used maternal and family roles to describe their leadership abilities. Mothering was the metaphor that defined their leadership.

A recent article in *USA Today* ,"Mothers Hone Leadership Skills on Career Breaks," highlights mothers' leadership strengths. I've believed this from the beginning of my mothering years.

According to the article, quiet, yet revolutionary migration is taking place. Women who have been running hard on the career track are taking a detour onto the mommy track. Harvard and Stanford business schools have studies to support this trend. In 2002, *USA TODAY*, reported that labor-force participation among new mothers dropped for the first time in nearly 25 years. Instead of this departure being seen as an embarrassing time out of the workforce, mothers are using this time to take advantage of mothering as a leadership opportunity.

This new movement shows women are re-creating their role as mothers and workers. Unlike generations past, women are beginning to realize their value both at work and in the home. Women are willing to depart from the working world so they can invest time in their families. Women are realizing the only way they can "have-it-all," is by making wise choices and viewing the long-term impact of their choices, which means *not even trying* to "do-it-all" at the same time.

During the past 30 years we have seen women make tremendous sacrifices in their personal lives to have successful careers. Now, women are trying to make more balanced choices. It's not a question of all or nothing in our work or personal lives, but how can we do it all over the long-term? More women are asking themselves this defining question. *"How can I recreate a life that's best for me and my family, playing by my own rules?"*

Decades ago, Eleanor Roosevelt noted that "a home requires all the tact and all the executive ability required in any business." Finally, we are understanding the richness and wisdom in those words.

Leadership Skills Transfer Between Home and Work

New and compelling evidence shows that the skills needed to manage in the workplace are similar to the skills needed to manage a household and children.

This evidence was the result of a study conducted by the Center for Research on Women at Wellesley College. Sixty female leaders ranging in age from 30 to 70 - including CEOs politicians and women with public profiles, such as poet Maya Angelou, were interviewed for the study.

Many of the women used maternal and family roles to describe their leadership or the leadership of other women. Mothering was the metaphor that defined leadership for these professionals. Read many of the leadership development books written by men and you'll find lots of sports and war metaphors. Women come from a different frame of reference and a different perspective.

Ask any mother who has a two-year-old and she will tell you mothering is a great training ground for conflict management and dealing with executives who are prone to temper tantrums. A mother who negotiates with an eight-year-old about the pros and cons of buying a Play Station™ has to have a real grasp on negotiation skills and problem solving. Only for Moms, the negotiations are much more intense with all the emotions, guilt and fear that come with the job. Women who are organizing play dates and their kids' schedules know more about time management than most. Mothers are learning about building collaborative relationships and managing differing personalities with their home teams every day.

The 7 VICTORY Leadership Skills© you can excel in are:

1. V-Visioning
2. I-Influential Communicating.
3. C-Change Management.
4. T-Team building.
5. O-Organization/ Planning
6. R-Resolving Problems and Conflict .
7. Y-because You are valuable!

MOMAGERS who learn these VICTORY Leadership skills can use them at home and in the workplace. So, although the revolution may be brewing quietly right now, just wait. Like a teakettle about to whistle, (or blow) these MOMAGERS are on the rise and will be a force to reckon with. As more mother-leaders move into top leadership and corporate jobs, a shift in society will occur. And while this shift may feel like it's long in coming, it doesn't have to be. If every mother in this country committed to voting and working toward the issues that are of primary importance to children and families, our country's "acceptable" policies in these areas would change rapidly and dramatically.

Isn't it time women are recognized, valued, and rewarded for our unique leadership abilities?

Over the past 18 years, I've held a variety of positions. I've been president of an international training company and consulted with numerous companies, a business executive for a fortune 100 company, a development director (fundraising executive for non-profit organizations), and a Mom.

During each assignment, I have been involved in leading projects or teaching teams of people how to reach peak performance and achieve goals. Whether it was visioning a new building or capital project for a university and rallying volunteers around the cause, visioning successful moves for corporate relocations, or visioning to raise healthy, responsible kids, the leadership skills to accomplish these goals have all been the same. Through years of leadership research, I believe leadership skills can be learned in the home *or* in the workplace and transferred between the two. I believe anyone can learn to lead effectively. It wasn't always this way and it took many heart-wrenching experiences for me to learn these lessons.

The contribution a mother makes in leading and guiding her children is one of the most significant and important contributions to society. Yes, other people are capable of watching our children, but who is the best person to *lead* our children? Each mother can be the best person to lead her children and family. There is a tremendous amount to teach our children and to learn from them. Being a leader is not always easy, but today it is a necessity. For some families, the dad may be the best person to care for the children and then he needs to lead in his own way. I think it's wonderful so many dads are staying home with children for some "leadership development" training. These dads have a much greater understanding of how difficult the job really is.

Some leaders are born, but most are bred. There's no magic secret to being a great leader. There are years of hard work and consistent effort and commitment needed. Some women already realize they have amazing leadership strengths and skills; some still do not.

My hope is to strengthen women so we all recognize the enormous responsibility we have leading our families, children and society into the future. This is no small task with all the forces in society trying to deflate our contribution. As Dr. Barnes, author of *Transformational Leadership* says, "Anybody can be a leader. Yes, there are male and female differences as to how we lead. A true leader is tough, idealistic, committed, persistent and strong, but not offensively strong."

Are you recognizing some of your leadership skills and opening your eyes to some others? Although you and I may not know each other, we have much in common. My hope is that reading this book will help you to discover how strong you – and all women – are, and how much more powerful and effective we can all become.

Chapter 2

Trust me, Love me, and Then I'll Follow You

The hand that rocks the cradle is the hand that rules the world.
-W. R. Wallace, A selection of writings from the field

When I stopped seeing my mother with the eyes of a child,
I saw the woman who helped me give birth to myself.
-Nancy Friday, Women on Top and My Mother/My Self

Trust is the super-glue of all relationships. You know how super glue holds everything together. It's amazingly strong. Once I accidentally got one tiny drop on my index finger and tried to get it off with another finger. Oh no! I thought my fingers were going to be stuck together for life! High levels of trust bind us together just like super-glue. Weak trust is like watered down glue. It runs, doesn't stick to anything, and makes a big mess with no connection.

Trust is the foundation of leadership. Understanding how we can develop a strong, solid foundation in our relationships is of vital importance to every leader, but especially Momagers. Let's use the analogy of a house. We spend so much time decorating and making our home a place of love and warmth that the most important part of the home often goes unnoticed – the foundation. It is made of concrete and steel. It is solid. The house stands upon it and it must be strong and endure for decades. If the foundation is weak, the house will crack and shift, and many other problems could surface. As the Dalai Lama revealed in his *Thoughts For The New Millennium*; "A loving atmosphere in your home is the foundation for your life."

How can we develop a trusting environment? To me, maintaining trust is a lot like keeping enough money in your purse. Every time we do something trustworthy, we deposit money into our wallet. (Deposits are made even when we just throw the change in the purse, absentmindedly, to be dug out at a much later time.) You can enjoy abundance in a relationship when there are plenty of deposits. When you have plenty of money, you can shop, shop, shop 'til you drop!

Every time you do something to break trust, it's like withdrawing money. If you keep spending and don't make any deposits, before you know it, you're broke and so is the relationship. Nobody is happy then. So, the trick is to keep depositing trust into your relationships and make withdrawals, only when they are absolutely necessary. When you *do* make a withdrawal, communicating, apologizing and trying to "fix" the problem helps you regain status. No credit cards are accepted in the trust arena.

During training sessions I ask the question "What do leaders do to make deposits or withdrawals? Here are a few of the responses:

Making Deposits

1. Keep promises. Do what you say you're going to do!
2. Tell the truth. Say what you mean, and mean what you say.
3. Respect others by the way you treat them. Treat others how you want to be treated.
4. Help others grow.
5. Invest the time and resources for projects that are in the best interest of your family or group.
6. Listen, really listen, with an attitude of openness and acceptance.
7. Have a vision and a plan for the future.
8. Support family members (co-workers and employees) and problem solve together.
9. Foster an environment of continuous learning. Let us fail and learn from our mistakes.

Making Withdrawals

1. Break promises.
2. Be inconsistent. Say one thing, and then do something else.
3. Lie. Even white lies can be a breach of trust.
4. Gossip.
5. Act disrespectful.
6. Be selfish. Put your own interests above what's best for the group.
7. Don't treat others how you want to be treated, or how they want to be treated.
8. Be pompous and superior with an "I know best" attitude.
9. Don't listen to new or different ideas. Say, "We always do it this way," or "I don't see how that can work."
10. Criticize, condemn, or complain instead of solving problems together.
11. Maintain a tense, "cover your bottom" environment where people are afraid to make mistakes.
12. When mistakes are made, show disapproval, yell, or demonstrate obnoxious or abusive behavior.

Fortunately, very few people go out of their way to do the things on the "Withdrawal" list and many people who read the list are aghast and can't believe anyone would ever behave in such an untrustworthy manner. And yet, these behaviors are demonstrated in families and in businesses every day.

Why is it so hard to trust? Typically, the relationship is overdrawn and we don't feel safe. There's a saying: "If I get burned once, shame on them. If I get burned twice, shame on me." When we get burned, it's hard to trust again. Depending on the situation, it could be that person has proven themselves untrustworthy, in which case we should be wary indeed. There is always a risk we can get hurt by trusting. Extending ourselves and being rejected in the past also make it hard to trust. We maintain trust and have a strong relationship when we continually make deposits into our "Trust Fund," and sparingly make withdraws.

To this day, I sit in chairs where my back faces the wall so I can see everyone else in a public place. A remnant of my Italian heritage is to be wary and cautious with trust. When someone earns trust, you can give it. You have to earn trust to receive it as well. Robert L. Woodrum, public relations advisor, wisely said, "You have the right to remain silent, but you can never, never lie or shade the truth."

Trust is Fragile, Handle with Care

Momagers know that trust is earned and that it is extremely difficult to reestablish once it's broken. This story demonstrates how fragile trust can be.

While living in London, one of the nicest traditions we practiced was "tea time." Many afternoons around 3:30 we would either go out to a tea shop or have tea and finger sandwiches or sweets at the office or home. I collected a few precious antique teacups. They were beautifully feminine, decorated with hand-painted flowers and had delicately curved handles with gold in-lay. These extravagant teacups were only used on very special occasions. I stored them on the top shelf of the cabinet high above a child's grasp. (Or so I thought).

One day, my then 3-year-old son Steven virtually scaled a wall to get a teacup and before I knew it, I heard a loud crash! One of my teacups shattered, never to be replaced. Should I just add it to his tab? He owes me at least $1,500.00 already if I count the broken VCR's, cabinet doors, and an assortment of dishes and vases. (Did I tell you he is very determined?) What Steven shattered was much more valuable than the cost to replace it, because like trust, the teacup was irreplaceable.

Like trust, this teacup could be put back together. I could painstakingly try to glue each broken piece back where it belonged. (Asking a mother of a toddler to do that would surely put her nerves to the test). Even with the best super-glue, guess what? It will never be the same. There will always be hairline cracks that are the remnants of the break.

When we break the trust in relationships, it can be mended, but it will rarely be the same as before the break. Relationships are damaged for the long-term if you smash them in too many pieces. Relationships can also be greatly strengthened when you withstand the storms together and make it through the tough times with mutual respect, trust, and forgiveness. Treat the trust and confidences of your children, family members, co-workers and friends in your highest regard. Trust is a most precious resource. Guard it wisely.

Forgiveness - Can We Start All Over Again?

We can learn from our mistakes and forge stronger bonds if we are willing and able to forgive and start over when we break a teacup. We need to apologize and truly mean it. All leaders make mistakes, and that includes Momagers. Watch and pay attention to how your family members respond when you apologize. If they see you admitting and learning from your mistakes, they will be committed to doing the same thing when they make mistakes. Refusing to play the "blame game" makes all the difference in the world.

What you learn from listening to and watching others will be invaluable. By paying attention to what people say and watching what they do, you will discover what they're made of. "Actions speak louder than words," the true adage proclaims. Our followers do what we *do*, not what we *say*.

Egotistical Vs. Humble Leaders

You can develop and maintain trust by putting aside your ego and being your authentic self. Egotistical leaders are well advised to rethink their demeanor. History shows that huge egos have contributed to the mediocrity and demise of plenty of companies and countries. Kim Chernin, author of 14 books, including *The Hungry Self*, said at a Women and Power dinner, "You sometimes pretend to be a man. Women have a different model of leadership that starts with fear. Women are a product of thousands of years of being inferior. Thousands of years of hearing, you are inferior. Go away. For women, becoming powerful happens step by step as we overcome fears to empowerment."

Words like humble, modest, reserved, gracious, and understated are commonly used to describe the men and women behind some of business' biggest success stories. These leaders usually shine the spotlight on their employees instead of on themselves. When graced with awards, they say things like "There are plenty of people in this company who could do my job better than me. I accept this award on behalf of all the employees who work tirelessly, they deserve this award."

Although great leaders are humble, they are not timid. Effective leaders have incredible self-confidence. As a Momager, you must believe in yourself, your family members, and your community to promote positive change, and convince others to follow the best path. This is where women can learn how to use a strong, yet convincing manner, to voice our opinions and speak up for what we truly believe in. Leading with an iron fist covered with a velvet glove is highly effective. When you have a driving vision, know what you want, and know what is best for your family and yourself, confidence develops. The passion your vision inspires makes it easier to stand up, speak up, and lead the way.

Mary Kay Ash was a perfect example of a leading lady who instilled trust. She founded Mary Kay Cosmetics at the age of 50 with only $5,000 in savings. From these humble personal and professional beginnings Ash helped build a company that now employs 400,000 consultants who generate about $2 billion in annual retail sales. She was named Lifetime TV's most influential woman in business in the 20th century. She died in 2001 but her lessons live on today.

"How people were treated was more important to me than profits and losses. That's why I say P&L means people and love. Of course I'm concerned about profits and losses. I just don't give them top priority," wrote Ash in her 1995 book *Mary Kay: You Can Have It All.*

Ash said, "A long time ago, I chose as my standard the Golden Rule: Do unto others as you would have them do unto you. My mother taught me this creed when I was a little girl and I have abided by it ever since. Being treated with respect is something every employee deserves, regardless of rank. Not only is it right, it has a positive effect on a company's overall success."

Mary Kay eloquently reminds us the only way to successfully manage all areas of our lives is to have our values and priorities in place. Her faith in God was the most important component in her life. She said, "I believe that each of us has God-given talents within us waiting to be brought into fruition. Each person is unique and special."

Ash knew how to instill a trusting environment. She worked to build her people up by letting them know she appreciated them. She motivated her salespeople with the highest commissions in the field. Her annual employee seminar spared no expense with prizes such as pink Cadillacs, diamond jewelry, and luxurious vacations.

She personally greeted all new employees at company orientation. She made a point to give all of her co-workers a cheerful greeting every day. She believed nothing is more contagious than enthusiasm, and nothing is more detrimental than negativity. "Eliminate a negative attitude and believe you can do anything. Replace 'if I can, I hope, I may' with "I can, I will, I must.'" Her goal in building people up was to help them build confidence in themselves. "Confidence stimulates your ability to perform," Ash said.

Mary Kay's policy of treating people right was not reserved for her employees. She made sure her salespeople were trained to give customers the best possible service and cater to their needs. "Being successful in business is a matter of giving the customer so much value, care, and attention, they would feel guilty even thinking about doing business with somebody else," Ash said. She truly believed that "The definition of successful people is simply ordinary people with extraordinary determination."

Mary Kay makes a great role model for Momagers. By following her leadership example, we can help to raise our children's self-confidence and show them how to treat others with care and respect.

Competence, Character, Connection, Consistency

Four elements to building trust are competence, character, connection with others, and consistency. As a leader, you must be competent and confident in your ability. Would you ever put your trust in someone who doesn't know what they're doing? Probably not. Others won't either. As a Momager, this is even more important because your children need to know they can trust you.

Competence

How do you show your family that you're competent and able to handle the job of Momager?

At work, competence is proven by successfully meeting the objectives of our position. When we apply for a job these questions come into main focus: Can you do the job? Can you perform well on the job? How do you prove this to others? Performance appraisals are a motivating factor (if done correctly) and can keep employees on track.

If you're a mom, you don't have performance appraisals to keep you on track and focused on your objectives. You have a higher authority to report to. You have your own performance appraisals and you are probably your toughest critic. Here are some questions that will help you clarify your competence.

1. Do I understand child development and the natural stages my children will experience as they grow up?
2. Do I enjoy my career as a Momager? (most of the time)
3. Do I confidently discipline and teach my children values?
4. Do I know about and approve of my children's education?
5. Do I know the best way for our family to communicate?
6. Do I know how we can solve problems easily and permanently?

I know this is a tough set of values and expectations. In fact, they're huge. But as Jaqueline Kennedy Onassis said, "If you bungle raising your children, nothing else matters much in life." Our children and families are that important.

As a Momager, always remember that there is a huge difference between being a leader through the position you hold and being a leader *by influence*. A true leader knows or seeks the answers to the questions previously listed. We grow into leaders and it takes years to develop our leadership style. I believe each mother is the best person to lead her children. However, it isn't something that just comes naturally. If there are any areas you feel you could grow in, those are areas you focus on.

How can you show your competence confidently?

Do a great job! Be a top performer and exceed expectations in your position. Loving what you do, and being good at it is the best indicator of competence.

Build a Network of Mentors

Network with other women to learn how they succeed. "Networking is the nonstop process of developing and maintaining quality relationships that are mutually beneficial," explains Andrea Nierenberg, author of *Nonstop Networking*.

As women, networking is a necessity. When networking, we want to focus on how we can support others and how we want to be supported.

Focus on the Five Ws:

Who?
What?
When?
Where?
Why?

Successful networkers know what they need for themselves, their family, and their business and they connect with others who can help. Keep a tickler file and jot down notes about the people you meet and their expertise. Networking is a two-way street because we are also helping others along the way. The give and take of these relationships broadens your connections. "The result is life enrichment and the empowerment to achieve your life goals," remarks Nierenberg.

As a Momager, a network of women is invaluable as you navigate your way through a maze of mothering challenges. Networking is even more necessary now, since extended family connections are more distant.

Families used to be physically closer to each other and the extended family supported the nuclear family. In Italy, India, Mexico and many other countries, extended families still live in the same house. Many Italian families have a three-story house with each floor built as a separate home. For example, Mom, Dad and their two daughters might live on the second floor, their son and his wife on the third floor, and Grandma and Grandpa on the first floor. In America, we are more isolated, so we don't have a built-in network of people to help us deal with daily life's assorted challenges. We need to work at building networks with other Momagers in our neighborhood and community. The saying, "It takes a village to raise a child," is truer now than ever.

I recommend making friends who are five to ten years older than you so you can learn from their expertise, and be ahead of the game in the parenting cycle. You'll know the normal phases (for you and your kids), if you hear it first-hand from experienced parents.

When I was living in England I was involved with the Northwood American Women's Club and now I'm involved in the Ministry of Mothers Sharing (M.O.M.S.) group through my church. In addition, six years ago I started a neighborhood Mom's group and we've all benefited and been blessed by our new friends and connections Since my family moved every few years, I have had the challenge and opportunity to network and make new associates and friends often. It's easy to do and it's fun. I've found that it's very helpful and rewarding to be involved in two or three groups, because we all have so much to share and each group is different.

There are major benefits of having a network of mentors. They support you, shorten your learning curve, and help you reach your objectives faster. Women support networks are growing every day. Check out your local library, the web, and your church and seek out other women. If you can't find a group that meets your needs or desires, start your own!

Commit to Life-long Learning

When I graduated from college I thought, "Alright, I'm finally done learning. Sixteen years was enough!" What happened the moment I entered the workforce with Merrill Lynch? I found out I knew nothing about my new career and I had a lot to learn! This situation has resurfaced with each new job. It seems like we know everything one day and then we start a new job or face a new situation and we feel like we don't know again. We start fresh with each new experience.

Stay current. Gain new insights and ideas. Never stop learning! Go back to school or read books and magazines. Get the training you need to acquire the skills you want to develop. Join associations and groups that support your learning.

When I was working with Merrill Lynch I read *Forbes, Business Week,* and *Tennis* magazines (to be well rounded). When I worked in the development field, I read *The Chronicle of Philanthropy, The Chronicle of Higher Education,* and *Wealth* magazine (to relate to the donors). As a business owner, I read *Entrepreneur,* a wide variety of training magazines, and the *Harvard Business Review* (to relate to my clients). As a Momager I read *Working Woman, Parents* magazine and a never-ending list of child development and family books (to relate to my children and husband). I share all these examples, not because I want to impress you (although now that I jot them down, I impress myself), but because there's power in knowledge. When we apply knowledge it becomes wisdom.

Let me applaud you for reading this book. You're continuing to learn and expanding your horizons. There's a wealth of information out there just waiting for you to explore. Learn - Grow - Stretch!

Be Prepared

Leaders are prepared and prepare relentlessly so they come across confidently and securely.

For Momagers, being prepared is an absolute necessity. Many women feel anxious during pregnancy because they fear they aren't prepared to have a baby or raise a child. All the responsibility that comes with leading a family can be overwhelming at first. Is that why we have nine months to "get-ready" for this momentous change in our lives?

The preparation never ends for Momagers. Look around and see the Moms with infants and toddlers. They are prepared with a bulging diaper bag filled with diapers, wipes, baby powder, extra bottles, formula, bibs, pacifiers, and toys. It takes Mom at least twenty minutes to pack the bag and get the baby dressed for a quick walk around the block. With kids' schedules, monitoring homework assignments, juggling tasks, and managing multiple responsibilities, Mom's hone their organization skills every single day. If you're not prepared, you'll feel like a steamroller is flattening you.

Look at moms of children in elementary school. They are busy managing every aspect of their kids lives by determining their development. They decide which activities their children will be involved with, what schools their kids will attend, and which classmates their children are allowed to visit and play with.

Moms of teenagers are leading the way by teaching independence, giving driving lessons, and helping their kids prepare for college entrance exams. Mothering never ends . . . really. Even though your years of direct influence end when your kids move out of the house, they will always look to you for approval and support.

Inform Others of Your Expertise

Have you ever noticed the way new college graduates treat their diplomas? They hold it up in the air and cheer, frame it, and proudly display it. But what happens after ten or fifteen years? It gets tucked away in a box and they assume people know their expertise. I encourage you to proudly display your credentials your entire life because they show others your experience and add credence to your reputation.

Keep in mind that there are lots of "credentials" that are worth displaying as Momagers and college degrees are not required for the job! Imagine a Momager display case filled with awards and representations of your greatest achievements. A thank you card from your six-year-old telling you you're a great Mom, the trophy you won in the 5K race (Mom's with little ones run all day!), the blue ribbon for the pie baking contest, and any awards or mementos that represent your role as a leader and Momager.

There are lots of ways to let our children and spouse know that we're competent and valuable. For example, my friend Julie tells her children about her coursework and current projects. She says sometimes she does this to give her kids a window to her world outside the home and sometimes she does it to convince herself of her own value. Either way, it works. (And sometimes she throws in how lucky they are to have her for a mom, lest they forget.) Taking stock of our experience and reminding ourselves of our worth, gives us confidence. One way to make sure our families and co-workers know what we've done is to *tell them.* Tooting our own horn for the right reason at the right time increases others' awareness of our contributions.

Surprisingly, people mistakenly assume that others recognize and appreciate their experience. Once people know we're competent, it makes discussions easier, encourages open problem solving, and establishes our expertise.

Continually Sell Yourself

We are all always selling ourselves. Although we don't usually call it selling, essentially, that's what we're doing. We're not selling products. We're selling our beliefs, ideas, and the projects we feel are important to accomplish. Whether we're in a meeting, talking to neighbors, having coffee with friends, or in playgroups, we're selling ourselves.

To "soft-sell" effectively, a little subtlety goes a long way. Before getting down to business, there is usually time for discussion. Tell an anecdote about successfully solving a problem similar to the one that's being considered. Or perhaps dinner or lunch is the time to mention years spent mastering a complex discipline -- not in a boastful way -- but in the normal give-and-take of conversation.

Character

"I have a dream that someday my children will live in a world where they are judged, not by the color of their skin, but by the content of their character." Martin Luther King's dream is just as needed today, as it was when he gave that famous speech. What does having content of character really mean?

We develop character by doing what is right and knowing the difference between right and wrong. We also have to be clear about what is the truth and what is a lie. Everything we do must be based on doing what is right. Sometimes that means standing up to criticism because we know deep within us we are doing the right thing.

We practice honesty when we speak truthfully and treat others fairly. We have integrity when we are honest with ourselves, holding to a code of moral values. There used to be a time in America when our word was our bond and our handshake was a "contract." Traditionally, our society counted on public figures such as athletes, politicians, and actors to be role models. Since the actions of so many of today's role models reveal a lack of honesty, it's even more important for us to be ethical role models. Who were your role models as a child? Who are your children's role models? Are they ethical and honest? There is a shortage of quality character leaders. As Betty Ford said, "Don't compromise yourself. You are all you've got."

When children are young and impressionable, tell them stories, read books, and watch movies about right and wrong and the difference between telling the truth and lying. There are some wonderful movies and books such as *Pinocchio, George Washington and the Cherry Tree,* and *The Lion King.* I also recommend a great poem called *Liar, Liar, Pants on Fire* by Miriam Cohen.

Many of us grew up with the motto, "Honesty is the best policy." If you changed your policy, would relationships be harmed? How would you feel if the tables were turned and someone close to you no longer valued honesty? Answering these questions reveals how fundamental and vital honesty is to relationships.

"Character contributes to beauty. It fortifies a woman as her youth fades. A mode of conduct, a standard of courage, discipline, fortitude and integrity can do a great deal to make a woman beautiful."

-- Jacqueline Bissett, Actress

Connection

AT&T had a great commercial and jingle. "Reach out and touch somebody's hand, this world's a better place if you can." We have to know and "touch" each other to develop trust. We have to continually earn trust.

My father has a saying he brought over from Italy. "Every mind has its own government." How true that has been throughout life! The trick is to find out what someone else's "government" believes.

Each person is unique and thinks differently. If we want to influence others, we need to know their beliefs, values, and needs. It means letting go of our own ego, and putting ourselves in other people's shoes.

1. Stay Connected.

Staying connected means committing time to and with others. Dr. James Dobson, Director of Focus on the Family highlights, "Parents average just five-and-a-half minutes of meaningful conversation with their children each day. Yet kids crave time with their parents."

My cousins in Italy spend much more time with their families than we do in the United States. When in Spain, I was so impressed by families going to lunch together. We're not talking about just the nuclear family either. We're talking about cousins, grandparents, and friends all included. It's common to see more than a dozen people sitting around a table, having lunch and enjoying siesta together. Why do they spend valuable work time, just visiting? They do it because they value family and want to stay connected. That means getting together every day or every week. When's the last time you got together with your family for a leisurely afternoon meal? And I don't mean the fifteen-minute shuffle. I'm talking about sitting around for a couple of hours really enjoying each other's company.

Do you work to live or live to work? It's an important distinction to make.

2. Regularly meet with your "team."

Whether you're a manager or a Momager, regular meetings are a must. If you work virtual, then phone or teleconference meetings work well. Daily meetings will help your team establish great synergy. When Rudy Giuliani was mayor of New York City he had his famous daily 8 a.m. team meeting. He said, "Open, honest communication keeps us connected." As a Momager, your role is to listen, ask plenty of questions, and motivate your team to work in unison on the same page. Consider starting each day with a short family breakfast "meeting," where you discuss the day's plans and objectives.

3. **Touch is a powerful tool to connect us with others, when appropriate.**

Have you ever watched politicians during election time? They try to touch as many people as possible with rousing speeches and handshakes. Why? The handshake has always been important in introductions and I encourage you to use this physical connection as much as you feel comfortable. There are three different types of handshakes.

- The traditional handshake. (connecting physically)

- The traditional handshake, plus the other hand surrounding the clasped hands. (getting closer)

- The handshake, plus the other hand clasping the other person's elbow. (really close now).

Each handshake has varying degrees of familiarity. When I have difficult people to deal with I will often touch their shoulder or arm to reassure them of my presence and support. Watch outgoing leaders; they often pat people's shoulders and make a physical connection. Make sure your motivation is honest or else this can be offensive.

Massage is an excellent form of touch that increases circulation and has many healing properties. Now, before you run out and book massage therapists for team meetings, let me just say, be diplomatic with plenty of modesty, please! Massage therapy can also be a wonderful treat for a Momager to give to herself and her family. Some therapists will even come to your home. Did you know John F. Kennedy used to take time off to get a massage before he gave a demanding speech? Massage relaxed him and helped him think clearly. It can help you, too. Try it, you'll really like it.

With children, it's amazing how a touch can soothe and wipe away all sorts of ailments from scraped elbows to bruised egos. Watch any mother with her children when they go to her with their boo boos. Quite often, the scratch or bump doesn't require medicinal treatment. However, the power to erase difficulties with a touch, kiss, or a little massage is amazing. Accompanied with reassuring words, like "You're going to be alright" is so transforming. Try it at home and work, diplomatically, of course.

Consistency

Leaders must be consistent in both good times and bad. Make sure others know what to expect from you. Be consistent in attitude, personality, and actions. If you're not consistent, others can't trust you. They'll keep asking, "Who is the real you?" "What should I believe?"

Working for an inconsistent boss taught me some valuable lessons. At the time, I was a project director for a private foundation and I thoroughly enjoyed making an impact by contributing millions of dollars to the community. (With her money, of course). Helping so many needy people was rewarding and deeply fulfilling. Working for a billionaire had plenty of advantages: a generous salary, splendid offices with teak wood desks, lavish luncheons at ocean-side restaurants, and high-profile acquaintances, just to name a few.

However, my boss had two very different faces. Every morning she had her "positive face" on. She was upbeat, cheerful, appreciative of all the workers, and would excitedly chat with us about our projects. After lunch, she had her "mean face" on. She was a totally different person. She was aggressive, demanding, expected everything done immediately and micro-managed.

After just four months, I quit! Working for her was like working for Dr. Jekyll and Mr. Hyde. Who was she and how was she going to behave next? The turnaround in her personality and change in her approach was too confusing, not to mention emotionally abusive. It was like working in a minefield. I never knew when the next mine would explode or where. Definitely not a trusting relationship or work environment. Considering how frustrating this experience was for me as an adult, can you imagine how upsetting and frightening it is for children when their parents are inconsistent?

Leaders entrust their team by being themselves, consistently. What is your personality and work style? Stick to it and even when you're under tremendous pressure or strain, work hard to remain consistent. We all know that when we're under stress and overwhelmed we have a tendency to over-react. If you feel stressed, give yourself a "time out" so you can regroup and work from a position of strength. Dale Carnegie advised us, "Rest *before* you're tired." If you wait until you're tired, it may be too late. A friend of mine said when her son was four years old and was being cranky because he was tired and in need of a rest, she'd say, "Michael, it sounds like you're ready for a nap." One evening, after a grueling day at work, she was snapping at her son and her husband as she made dinner. She said she didn't even realize she was doing it until her son suggested, "Mommy, it sounds like you're ready for a nap."

Momagers know what a precious resource sleep is. Ask a new mother what she wants most, and sleep will always be in the top three. Pam Brown, Author of *To A Very Special Mother in Law* eloquently said, "Mothers are the pivot on which the family spins. Mothers are the pivot on which the world spins." We can be much more consistent if we are well rested, peaceful, and healthy.

As a leader, your mood and work style set the tone for the rest of the team. During the day, check in with yourself and see how you're doing. Your mood rubs off on other people so you need to make sure you remain positive and focused.

Consistently ask yourself: What do I need today? What does my family need? What does my work need? Those questions guarantee you're working on the priorities of the three most important areas of your life. And guess what? Doing this frees you from taking on too much and dictates what you say yes to and what to say no to. As women, if we continually ask ourselves these questions, we will be empowered to follow our conscience and attend to our highest priorities, instead of letting others control our actions and decisions.

Consistent Leaders are Confident and Humble

Leaders walk a fine line between having a high level of confidence and being egotistical. On the one hand, leaders must believe in themselves and their power to achieve goals. On the other hand, they must be humble and recognize the power of teams.

America was founded on a rugged individualistic mentality. The pilgrims broke away from England because they wanted freedoms the Mother Land wouldn't allow. The pilgrims had to be brave, adventurous, and confident the new world would be better. The pilgrims soon discovered they had to work together as a team or they would all die. Like the early Americans, we need a strong confidence in ourselves, and enough humility to do what's best for the team. When leaders let their egos get in the way, the good of the team is nearly always compromised.

A leader realizes every single person involved in a project or family has a unique contribution. Leaders capitalize on the strengths and passions of each person to create synergistic teams.

Establish Routines and Order, Yet be Flexible

When an environment is orderly, people know what to expect, can adjust to changes, and be more flexible. They know where to find things and when events are planned. Mothers have to keep track of multiple schedules, negotiate play dates, and keep the family's calendar. I say, "If you want to get things done, ask a busy person. If you want to get things done fast and right, ask a mom."

Moms are some of the most efficient and organized workers because their time is at such a premium and they are managing multiple priorities much of the time. Heck, most new moms can make dinner, carry a baby on their hip, and talk on the telephone, all at the same time.

Momagers are flexible! Erin Shriner, psychologist and mother of two, says "We have to be flexible because the kids are always changing and you never know who's going to puke on the way to school or practice." Keeping your home and office orderly and having set routines is best for everyone. Without them, you waste time and energy and chaos erupts.

I grew up in a home that had very little order. As a child living in a disorganized home with four siblings, life was very difficult and bordered on chaotic. Having a mother with A. D. D. (undiagnosed and untreated) was challenging. However, what it *did* teach me was how to organize chaos, which is a very important and useful skill. (See how we can even learn from the challenging times?)

One cold and wintry Christmas season when I was eight years old, my Girl Scout troupe was having a gift exchange. My sister Carlene and I were just 11 months apart in age, so we were very close growing up and in the same troupe. A few weeks before the event we told Mom we had to bring a wrapped present. "OK, we'll get something nice." Mom said. A week elapsed and still no presents. A few days before the event we reminded Mom again. "OK, OK, yes, I'll get the gifts. How about some pink bubble bath?" she asked. "Sure," we said, "get the kind that smells like roses."

Well, the day of the exchange arrived. At 3:30 p.m. we bounced off the bus, ran home, and you guessed it – no presents. The meeting was at 4 p.m. and we were getting nervous. My Mom hurriedly ran to the store, but didn't return home in time for us to go to the meeting.

In the meantime, Carlene was creative and determined to bring a gift. We searched the house for something she could give away, something that wasn't too tattered. An old wallet was a perfect gift (or so we thought). We wrapped the package with some aluminum foil and a big white bow. The wallet looked cheerful (certainly shiny) and we were convinced no one would be the wiser as to its previous use. At 3:55, Carlene and I walked to the meeting. She carried the lovely package and I walked along empty handed and heavyhearted.

My stomach was in knots as the meeting began. I told the leader I couldn't participate because I didn't have a gift. As the other girls selected their gifts I was horrified and gripped with fear. Who was going to get the old, worn out, wallet? Would the girls find out who put the ugly wallet in and hate us forever?

Meanwhile, Carlene opened her gift and got an amazing make-up kit. We were so excited to share the make-up! We were giggling and chatting away about how beautiful we would look with rosy

46

cheeks. We grew up rather poor and weren't allowed such a luxury as make-up.

Then we heard a cry from Shelly. The dreaded moment had arrived. Shelly had opened the wallet, started crying, and was disgusted. To make a long story short, the Girl Scout leader intervened. Carlene had to give up the make-up and take home her shabby wallet.

It was then I realized the damage being dishonest and unorganized inflicts upon others. All the pain, confusion, and difficulty could have been avoided if Mom just planned in advance and if my sister would have been honest.

Be Prepared

To this day, I'm usually over prepared for a meeting or presentation, having practiced it many, many times. I buy presents months in advance and have a "present box" in my closet filled with birthday gifts, spare candles, housewarming gifts, teacher gifts, and miscellaneous items that make great impromptu presents. The gift box gives me security and peace and extra time so I don't have to run out at the last minute. When we are orderly, we can be more flexible.

For presentations, I am usually an hour early and meticulously practice every sentence. It's common for me to "rehearse" a day's training program in front of a mirror, children, stray animals, or anyone who will listen to me. Why? To be prepared. To be so confident in what I will say that when difficulty or chaos arises, (which it oftentimes does) I can be flexible and "look" flawless.

If you're wondering if my mother is organized now, the answer is no, and it's okay. She's getting better. We laugh about our differences. Through the years I have bought her an array of planners, address books, and organization tools. To this day, she'll call me in Ohio from Connecticut to ask for her niece's phone number who lives just ten minutes away. Ahhhh - we have to accept people where they are and help them grow. Wouldn't it be a boring world if we were all the same? Differences really do add diversity to life. Being organized helps you and your children to know what to expect, and when.

The opposite extreme is the household or office that is so orderly, there's no room for flexibility or creativity. In the movie, *My Big Fat Greek Wedding* we laughed when we saw the plastic on the furniture and the perfectly vacuumed carpet in the room that no one is allowed to enter. This type of environment doesn't let people relax enough to be creative. People are so concerned about making everything "look perfect" and are so focused on appearances that they lose valuable time for relationships and having fun.

Somewhere in between the "messies" and Martha Stewart perfect order, (which isn't so perfect after all) there is a balance. An orderly home allows us to feel comfortable, more peaceful, and promotes efficiency. It saves us time and energy. Just think about how much time you spend if you can't find an important document? You waste so much time trying to dig it out of the papers or folders (or garbage cans), where you think it might be buried. When we are organized we can focus on the relationships and not be distracted by the mess.

Wendy McDonough, a health-care executive and mother of three, occasionally works from home and cleans up the living room before she can work on her computer. Many women feel attached to their surroundings and can think more clearly when order exists.

Women Have to Trust Each Other

For women to move forward, we must be able to trust, support, and rely on each other. Kay Baily Hutchison, Senator from Texas, remarks, "We must value every choice a woman can make. The value of community builders is real!"

It is encouraging to see so many networking and mentoring groups for working women. When we know each others' stories, challenges, and opportunities we can rise together. There are already some MOMAGER support groups for mothers who are staying home full time or part time. There still isn't enough support, so consider starting a Momager group in your community, rather than waiting for someone else to lead the charge.

There is still a deep and divisive separation between the worlds of work and home. Working women tell me they love their work and yet feel deficient compared to stay-at-home moms. Stay-at-home moms feel like they may be wasting valuable work time compared to their working counterparts. We must stop comparing and support all women, regardless of their working status. Let's rely on each other more and appreciate each other more.

Trust begins with each of us, proving our trustworthiness, and reaping the rewards of empowered relationships. We really do need each other. "It is the wrong notion that female power can only be manifested outside the home," says Elaina Richardson-Editor in Chief of *Elle* magazine. If we are in a position of power, we have a responsibility and a unique opportunity to help our sisters.

Trust is crucial to all relationships. Trust yourself. Trust your intuitions. Trust other women.

Let others trust you.

Chapter 3

V – Visioning. How Can You Have Crystal Clear Vision?

"Without a vision, the people perish."
The Bible-Proverbs 26:18

Have you ever been bombarded with a hundred important things to do all at once? Your daughter has soccer practice, your son has piano lessons, your husband's late from the office, everyone's looking for food and expecting you to provide it. Yes, they're starving, again. A friend really needs to talk and you want to listen, but don't know how you can fit her in. Your mind's racing around the five things left on your "to-do" list. Is it too much to fit in just 15 minutes of exercise? I mean, if Oprah can do it with her busy schedule . . .

Everyone tugs at you. Everyone needs you, day in and day out --
now. Maybe you're so caught up in living day-to-day or even minute-to-minute that you haven't had time to think or dream. What do you want? Somehow, what you truly want and desire keeps getting pushed to the bottom of the list. Deep inside, you know things aren't quite right. A sense of dissatisfaction nags at you. Something's not right. But what? And how do you make it better?

If you've ever felt like this, you can benefit from having a clear vision and purpose. There's hope! And, there are ways to tap into your inner core so you can handle what's most important to you and feel okay about saying no to the others.

The following is a three-step plan that will help you get in touch with your vision, values, and priorities. Once you are clear, you can set goals and achieve them.

The Three-step Plan includes:

<u>Step One:</u>
Defining and understanding your vision and purpose

<u>Step Two:</u>
Determining your values

<u>Step Three:</u>
Setting your top priorities

Step One

Define Your Vision and Purpose

So, what is a vision? I'm not talking about a nebulous sighting that a fortune-teller might share. The simplest definition of vision is "to see." When we see things clearly with our eyes we have good vision. Think of the eye doctor's chart. Can you see those tiny letters on the bottom row? I swear those characters aren't really letters at all. It's usually easy to see the big, bold letters, but the tiny letters elude us unless we have crystal-clear vision. Sometimes we need glasses, contacts, or even surgery to see well again.

If you want to see clearly and plan what you want to accomplish, you need to have a vision -- a mental picture of what you want to create. A vision is a mental image and purpose for a project. Your life is your longest project. And I mean long. A vision contains what you want to accomplish with a project, family, or community group. Literally think about what you want to "see" happen. This is vision. Taking the long-term view about what you want to do or what needs to be done to ensure a project's success is a positive vision.

What is your vision for your life? What do you want to see happen with your family, business, team, or community group? Answers to these questions take some thought. Every person and team shapes their future by creating a vision and purpose.

Whether your vision is constructing a new building, running a marathon for charity, starting a new program, publishing a book, opening a wellness center, or raising strong and responsible children, you must have a vision of what you are trying to accomplish.

Think about when a child wants to build a snowman from newly fallen snow. What happens? The child imagines what the end result will look like and then tries, tries, and tries to build it according to the vision. She imagines a snowman with three round balls of snow, two eyes, a carrot nose, a red hat, and the striped scarf. She begins building based on the end result that she sees in her mind. If she gets tired midway, then she starts to ask (beg) friends for help in a persuasive way. You know what I mean if you've ever been coaxed by a child's warm, expressive eyes. "Pleeeeeze," she pleads. She continues to persist based on her vision of the end result. Along the way, the snowman may change in detail, but the "big picture" stays the same.

Good leaders have a clear vision of the future and are totally committed to their group and the completion of their goals. To define your vision, ask the following questions: What does the end result look like? What do I/we want to accomplish?

When I was a college development director our leadership team was responsible for visioning the future of the school. During strategic planning sessions, all the schools leaders would brainstorm this question, "What is the best thing for the students and school in the next five to ten years?" In one particular session, we determined that the college needed a better student sports center.

An architect completed drawings of a potential sports facility. The drawings and vision were beautiful with a swimming pool, tennis courts, weight room, and areas for fitness classes. A detailed drawing of both the outside and inside of the building had to be done so everyone could "see" what we would build.

Then we began selling that vision to potential donors. We always showed the donors the drawings of the facility and explained why the need existed and how their money would be spent. They rallied behind the project once they could envision how their money would help the students. The donors who made the largest contributions were motivated by the idea of securing the long-term vision of leaving their legacy by having a building or room named after them.

The same concepts apply to family visioning. Parents create the vision for their families. Your children are the legacy you are sending into the future -- complete with your name and imprint.

• What type of family life/environment do you want to create?

• What type of people do you want your children to be?

• After 18 years of service, what do you hope to have accomplished with your children? (By then, they should be adults and ready to leave home, right? Please, reassure me that this is true!)

So many of us focus on living day-to-day without thinking of our own purpose or our family's purpose. I challenge you to answer the questions above and think of your role in the family as one of leadership. To be successful, we need to commit ourselves to the things that really matter to us. For moms to stay on course, we need to know what type of culture we want to create in our homes. When my husband and I looked at our family this way, we determined our vision.

The process of discovering and re-designing your vision can take months or years. Do you know what our vision was for our family when all three children were under four years old? It can be summed up in one word: SURVIVAL! For the kids -- and for us. Getting all the kids out of diapers and walking seemed like a distant dream and an unattainable long-term vision. For years, Bob and I yearned for them just to all walk, talk, and go to the bathroom by themselves! I suppose you could call those initial visions short-term rough drafts. Now, our vision is: To guide our children to be loving, self-sufficient and responsible adults who will contribute to the well being of society. (We really don't want to raise thugs!)

Many women start using visioning skills as soon as they consider getting pregnant, or as soon as they find out their daughter is thinking about conceiving. The following anonymous story found on the internet, brings this idea to life.

My daughter and I were having lunch when she casually mentioned she and her husband were thinking of "starting a family." She said, "We're taking a survey," half-joking. "Do you think I should have a baby?"

"It will change your life," I said, carefully keeping my tone neutral.

"I know," she said," no more sleeping in on weekends, no more spontaneous vacations..."

But that's not what I meant. I looked at my daughter, trying to decide what to tell her. I wanted her to know what she would never learn in childbirth classes. I wanted to tell her that the physical wounds of child bearing will heal, but that becoming a mother will leave her with an emotional wound so raw that she will forever be vulnerable. I considered warning her that she will never again read a newspaper without asking "What if that had been MY child?" That every plane crash, every house fire will haunt her. That when she sees pictures of starving children, she will wonder if anything could be worse than watching her child die.

I looked at her carefully manicured nails and stylish suit and thought that no matter how sophisticated she was, becoming a mother would reduce her to the primitive level of a bear protecting her cub. That an urgent call of "Mom!" will cause her to drop a soufflé or her best crystal without a moment's hesitation. I felt I should warn her that no matter how many years she has invested in her career, she will be professionally derailed by motherhood. She might arrange for childcare, but one day she will be going into an important business meeting and she will think of her baby's sweet smell. She will have to use every ounce of her discipline to keep from running home just to make sure her baby is all right.

I wanted my daughter to know that everyday decisions would no longer be routine. That a five-year-old boy's desire to go to the men's room, rather than the women's, at McDonald's will become a major dilemma. That right there, in the midst of clattering trays and screaming children, issues of independence and gender identity will be weighed against the prospect that a child molester may be lurking in that restroom. However decisive she may be at the office, she will second-guess herself constantly as a mother.

Looking at my attractive daughter, I wanted to assure her that eventually she will shed the pounds of pregnancy, but she will never feel the same about herself. That her life, now so important, will be of less value to her once she has a child. That she would give it up in a moment to save her offspring, but will also begin to hope for more years -- not to accomplish her own dreams, but to watch her child accomplish his or hers. I wanted her to know that a cesarean scar or shiny stretch marks will become badges of honor.

I knew my daughter's relationship with her husband would change, and not in the way she thought. I wished she could understand how much more you can love a man who is careful to powder the baby or who never hesitates to play with his child. I wanted her to know that she would fall in love with him again for very unromantic reasons.

I wished my daughter could sense the bond she would feel with women throughout history who have tried to stop war, prejudice, and drunk driving. I hoped she would understand why I can think rationally about most issues, but become temporarily insane when I discuss the threat of nuclear war to my children's future.

I wanted to describe to my daughter the exhilaration of seeing your child learn to ride a bike. I wanted to capture for her the belly laugh of a baby who is touching the soft fur of a dog or a cat for the first time. I wanted her to taste the joy that is so real it actually hurts.

My daughter's quizzical look made me realize that tears had welled up in my eyes. "You'll never regret it," I finally said. I reached across the table, squeezed my daughter's hand and offered a silent prayer for her, and for me, and for all of the mere mortal women who stumble their way into this most wonderful of callings. This blessed gift from God. That of being a Mother.

You can see how this mother was visioning all the changes her daughter would experience as a result of becoming a mother and how that role would change the rest of her life.

Step Two

Determine Your Values

Once your vision is clear, clarify your values. As leaders, we want to think about how we are going to see the vision become a reality. We have to get everyone working on the same page. We have to rally the troops. Getting people rallied around a cause or project requires each Momager to identify her values and her family's values.

Leaders who are committed to the success of their teams create mission statements to keep the group on course. In business, the company needs to make a financial profit for shareholders. In non-profit organizations, that means providing services that help and profit the community. For government, it means keeping the people in the country safe and economically secure. (Yes, that's what they're supposed to do.) For schools, it means teaching students information they need to grow intellectually and prepare for life.

Successful groups have clear values and people know what those values are. When I worked with Merrill Lynch, I really appreciated their principles. These principles reflect the company's values and guide business decisions and employee behavior.

Merrill Lynch's corporate values or guiding principles are:
Client Focus
Respect For The Individual
Teamwork
Responsible Citizenship
Integrity

With raising responsible children, instilling enduring values is critical. So, what do you value? As a mother, it's important to look at the end of your child-rearing years. (I'm guaranteed, it really does end some day.)

Ask yourself these questions:

• What memories do you want your children to cherish?

• What values do you want to instill in them?

• What experiences do you want them to have so they grow healthy and strong?

In order to project that far into the future it's critical we think of basic eternal values. Think about values that are most important to you. How are you going to instill them in your children before they leave home? Think of what you expect from the next generation of leaders and teach your children those values.

The Top 10 Core Values for Teams/Families

- Value #1   Honesty
Honesty is being truthful with other people, institutions, and yourself. We develop inner strength and confidence by being truthful, trustworthy, and having integrity.

- Value #2   Commitment and Determination
Commitment and determination are our binding pledge to our ideals, our work, and each other through thick and thin, good times and bad. We hold high standards for family, work, and ourselves. We remain loyal to our beliefs, country, family, and friends. We have the determination to keep trying until we achieve our goals.

- Value #3   Courage
With courage, we can face difficult or fearful situations and do what's right. Courage means having the strength and boldness to influence others and to say, "no," and mean it. Being true to convictions, even when they're unpopular, is being courageous.

- Value #4   Cooperation and Teamwork
Teamwork means combining our energy with others to work toward a common goal. When we cooperate, we can accomplish tasks through understanding and peaceful means.

- Value #5   Self-reliance and Self-discipline
Self-reliance is defined by being a unique individual and trusting your knowledge, experience, and talents to make good decisions and choices. Taking care of our physical and mental health and wisely managing our finances are all forms of self-discipline.

- Value #6   Respect
We show respect by admiring and appreciating life, authority, nature, and people. Being respectful means being polite and courteous.

• Value #7   Responsibility

When we are responsible, we are trustworthy and dependable -- someone others can count on. Being responsible for ourselves or others means we're accountable for our actions and take responsibility for the consequences of our choices.

• Value #8   Love and Understanding

Showing love and understanding means giving kind, personal care to ourselves, family, friends, and even enemies. It means being willing to sacrifice for others and seeking to understand others.

• Value #9   Patience

Patience is the ability to delay gratification and endure the waiting calmly.

• Value #10   Integrity and Justice

Being fair in work and play, knowing right from wrong, and doing the right thing are all aspects of living with integrity and justice. Obedience to the law and higher authorities is a demonstration of our integrity

Other values include:

Authenticity	Education	Loyalty
Balance	Financial Freedom	Physical Fitness
Beauty	Gratitude	Spirituality
Career	Humor	

With a clear sense of shared vision and values, we can consistently hold ourselves and others accountable to certain ways of behaving. Some pretty high standards can be established based on shared values. Remember that values are caught, not taught.

What really challenges Momagers is how to consistently instill these values over the long haul. First of all, it's important for you and each member of your family to prioritize the previous list of values. For instance, do you value honesty more than responsibility? Rank the values in the order of most important to least important. Once you determine which values are most important to you and your partner, you have a foundation for sharing and demonstrating those values to your children.

As a consultant, I see some organizations that live out their values, and others that do not. When there is a conflict, the true value of the person or group comes out in the actions and emotions of the people. When we say that we hold a certain value, but don't demonstrate that value in our actions, we have a value discrepancy. Some people refer to this as being out of integrity with ourselves and with others.

Here are some examples:

Honesty

What's the difference between the truth and a lie? Help your family members to see the long-term effects of dishonesty by presenting them with situations that show the difficulty of misrepresenting the truth.

For example, let your children know that if they take credit for someone else's work, they are stealing that person's ideas and possibly his or her chance of getting a good grade. Explain that if they cheat on a quiz, they won't really learn the information and they may need the information on a test again or in real life. (Imagine that?) Show them if they stand on their tiptoes in the doctor's office while getting measured this year, next year it may look like they haven't grown much or at all. The doctor will wonder why they've stopped growing. Pinocchio's nose grew when he lied, but when we lie; we shrink smaller in other people's eyes.

Commitment and Determination

There would be no great inventions or progress without commitment and determination. As a society, we wouldn't have telephones, cars, electric lights, the vaccine for polio, indoor plumbing, or the ability to travel by airplane – just to name a few. Commitment allows us to bond with friends or a project despite difficulties, disagreements, and disillusionment. When the going gets tough, the tough get going! Just like the itsy bitsy spider, we must try, try, and try again if we want to meet goals and achieve our vision for the future.

Think about a project you've worked on for a long time. How did you feel when you were finished? Happy? Proud? A sense of accomplishment? Co-workers and children need to learn that each project requires thinking through from the beginning and completing the project is part of the process. Letting others quit denies them the opportunity to experience the pride and satisfaction that come with finishing.

Teaching your children how to grow plants, care for pets, and solve their own problems takes time and a long-term commitment. When disagreements occur, instead of always intervening, encourage your children to negotiate a peaceful resolution. Our willingness to work things out shows our commitment to each other.

Courage

Acting with courage is difficult because we all experience fear. The question is how do we face it? Fear can immobilize us or we can use our mind and body to help control the fear. Being courageous means feeling the fear and acting appropriately.

One of the biggest fears people have is public speaking. I've often been asked, "How do you stay so calm and relaxed while speaking?" "Do you get nervous?" Yes! Before almost every speech, I'm nervous. Sir Laurence Olivier used to empty the contents of his stomach before his stage performances. Winston Churchill, one of history's greatest orators, suffered such stage fright that he'd rehearse his speeches obsessively. Luciano Pavarotti, the great tenor, said it was concentration, more than voice, that made a singer great. "I like 'nervous' in a performance," he once said.

We assume that fear leads to failure. Not so. When fear doesn't paralyze, it can be a motivator. High achievers see fear as a necessary evil, or a valuable ally. Is it going too far to ask you to think of fear as a friend who is telling you when something is of utmost importance? We're scared for a reason. Fear tells us when to be alert. Improved focus is fear's most valuable byproduct. We pay full attention to the task at hand when we're afraid. It can work to our benefit to face our fear almost like a rocket uses jet fuel. It propels us into new and unknown territory and is necessary for us to grow.

You can instill courage in the face of fear by slowly helping others build strategies for being courageous. When children are allowed to experience consequences for their actions they begin to face their fears. Encourage children to talk about their fears. Sometimes putting them into words is all that is needed to put fears at rest. Try to help kids identify the differences between real and imagined fears. Use puppets and play that allow kids to express their fears.

When your children express their fear, help them think of ways to be brave. For example, if a child's afraid of the dark, he might turn on a nightlight, or play soft music before he goes to bed. Or, if she's afraid of water, enrolling her in swim lessons might help. Help children stand up for what they believe in. And tell them how proud you are that they can hold to their convictions.

Cooperation

American society was built on the cooperation of the pilgrims. Communities were established by combining resources. Barn raisings, quilting bees, cooking together, and bartering were all ways of supporting and relying on each other. As we've moved from an agrarian society through the industrial revolution and into the electronic and digital age, the way we interact with each other has changed. But the importance of cooperation, working together, and relying on one another, remains the same.

We know we get the best results through the efforts of many. Combined personality types, talents, and knowledge strengthen productivity.

Remember this children's song?
The more we get together, together, together,
The more we get together, the happier we'll be,
Cause your friends are my friends
and my friends are your friends.
The more we get together, the happier we'll be.

"Sharing" has been one of the hardest lessons to watch my children learn. As soon as they learned, "It's mine," they faced an internal struggle between what they would share and what they wouldn't. The lesson of sharing and cooperating is a difficult value to instill and the current proliferation of materialism in our "throw away" society makes it even more challenging.

Here's what you can do:

Brainstorm a list of things that you can't do by yourself. Once you've made your list, look at the jobs or activities that you and your friends or family can do together. At work and at home, practice taking turns: I do this for you, you do that for me. People must know they can rely on each other. When we forge successful partnerships, everyone wins.

It may seem like a lot of work to instill values and initially it is. But the rewards for families who have clear values and ethics and who know how to behave and what is acceptable or unacceptable, are rich and plentiful. Break down instilling values into manageable baby steps and you will see major differences in how people act. An excellent resource is *Teaching Your Children Values* by Linda and Richard Eyre. They suggest focusing on one "value of the month" for a year. Different methods, stories, games, and other ideas are highlighted with their values.

No matter how hard we try, sometimes we will be "off-course." However, with visioning, good leadership, and faith we greatly increase our chances of success. (And isn't it better than the alternative -- i.e. chaos?)

As parents and leaders of the family, we have an awesome responsibility to have a vision and mission for our families. Our vision is like a pilot's flight plan. If we have not charted our course, the chance of ending up where we want to go is slim to none. Worse, when we get off-course, we run a greater risk of ending up in dangerous territory or crashing. Since there are so many other voices and influences trying to mold our kids, we must be diligent in our effort to make the biggest, most lasting impact.

Mission Statements

A mission statement explains what your purpose is and the contributions you are going to make. To create a mission statement, look at what your family is all about and ask some fundamental questions.

- Why do you and your family exist?
- What is your unique contribution?

Mission statements explain what is important based on your values and priorities. They also create a unifying force among family members. The important thing is that the mission statement represents everyone in the family. A powerful mission statement brings your family together, inspires each member of the family, and unifies everyone. It is a statement that clarifies the direction in which you are moving.

Once your vision and values are clear, create your mission statement.

Here are a few examples:

"To ignite the spark of faith and love in the lives of all who know me, family first."

Glenna Salsbury, author of *The Art of the Fresh Start*

"To get our kids through childhood happily and safely, while remaining married. We want our own goals to fit into the family goals so everyone is fulfilled."

The Fulford Family

"We will love, respect, and have confidence in each other."

The Kreider Family

"We love God, ourselves, and each other, and strive to support one another."

The McDonough Family

Your mission statement may have several drafts and evolve and change over time. For two years I wanted to create a mission statement, however we never seemed to find the time. Or should I say we never *made* the time. Finally, an opportunity presented itself. We were planning to drive to Florida -- a 23-hour trip that translated to four full days in the car. "Aha!" I thought. This is it! I'm going to get everyone involved and we're going to do this. So, the kids all gave their input and by the time we came home, the first draft was done! We reviewed it again two weeks later and everyone gave input again. Now, the statement is on the front of the fridge held secure with a magnet and we use it as a guiding force for our family.

Our family mission is expressed through this statement:

"Our family is faithful, loving, and respectful. We accept each person's uniqueness. We treat each other how we want to be treated. We seek to understand and solve our problems. We serve each other and the community. Our home is an orderly place where family and friends find joy, comfort, and peace. We grow in love, learning, and laughter. All family members strive to grow to their fullest potential. We strive to be healthy and balanced in the following areas: mind, body, and spirit."

The statement sets the course for our family and holds everyone accountable. Since we have the sentence about orderliness, guess whose job it is to keep the house clean? Not just Mom's anymore. Yippee! Every single person is responsible to the family so every person contributes. Believe me, chores are no longer the drudgery they once were because of this family document. Everyone agreed how important orderliness was and poof! It's everyone's job.

I suggest that you review your mission statement once a year and change it when necessary. As you can see, the vision or mission statement doesn't have to be a lengthy document. It could be just a word, or phrase, or even artwork. Anything that will keep you and your family on track and focused on the important things will work.

Step Three

Setting Your Top Priorities

"Imbalance keeps us moving. If you can learn to laugh whenever you trip, teeter, or fall, you'll start to appreciate how much a misstep can teach you."
- Author unknown

Rather than helping you to get more done, I am encouraging you to do more of the important things and less of the unimportant ones. This means knowing when to say yes, and when to say no, and not feeling guilty. Ahhhh.... who will admit to being good at saying no?

People often ask me how I stay balanced. Well, I had to be totally off-balance and burnt out (a few times) before I understood the wisdom of balance. One day I knew I met "life burnout" when I had to be out of the house at 6:30 a.m. for a corporate training program. My son Steven was complaining of a tummy ache and proceeded to lose the contents of his stomach on my "dry-clean only" suit five minutes before I was supposed to leave. I had been up twice during the night and felt like all I was doing was rushing, rushing, rushing for years. I kept hearing myself say to friends, "Things will slow down in the spring, fall, winter." Whatever the next season was. I had visions of slowing down, but the reality continued to elude me. Everything had to be done perfectly and on time or else chaos would break out. That day, I snapped and realized I couldn't do it anymore. Now, after letting go and re-prioritizing many work, home, and volunteer commitments, I am much more proactive about how I invest my time and have learned how to continually balance.

If you're like most moms, the list of things to do is endless. Work commitments, family schedules, hobbies, exercise, church, and volunteering all tug at our time like a receding tide. Balancing is a lot like the tide, sometimes it's in and you feel great and elated and life is wonderful. Sometimes the tide is out and you are unbalanced and can't seem to reach what you want. We all have the capacity to balance ourselves, to set our own priorities and create our own agendas. Our influence over ourselves can be far stronger than any other influence.

Tips to Help You Prioritize

Admit to yourself that you can not do everything today! Andrea Mitchell, NBC Correspondent says, "We think we can do it all – You can't do that –- I have struggled with that every day."

Our culture has placed such unrealistic expectations on moms. With the dawn of feminism, some pretty unreasonable expectations have surfaced. "Bringing home the bacon and frying it up in a pan" is a crock! Most women who are bringing home the bacon are ordering out or picking up fast food. Let's get real! We have to do what we can and stop feeling guilty about what we can't.

Ask yourself the question: "What are my priorities now?

1. Self (and your relationship to God)
2. Family
3. Work/Profession

It's important to rank these three areas and then compare how much time and effort you really give each one. For instance, 15 years ago when I was single, I gave 80 percent of my time to work, 10 percent of my time to family, and 10 percent of my time to myself. Now that I'm the mother of three school-age children, my priorities are 1. Self, 2. Family, and 3. Work. And my daily life activities reflect these priorities.

We feel unbalanced if we really don't know our priorities and how much weight we want to assign each one. Sit quietly and think about your priorities; your answers will surface. Life balance means finding an equilibrium between the outer success of achievement and the inner success of family and personal growth.

When we reflect on these three categories, we realize they are BIG. We need to further prioritize and the wheel of life can help us do just that.

Wheel of Life

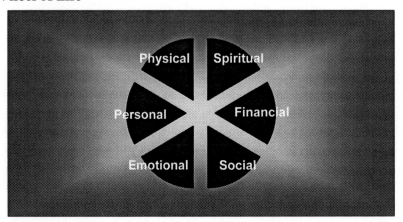

Think about the "wheel of life" containing these six categories:

1. Physical
2. Personal
3. Emotional
4. Social
5. Financial
6. Spiritual

How would you rate yourself in each of these areas on a scale of 1-10? 1 being dissatisfied to 10 being fabulous. Start with yourself. Then do the same with your family members. Take some time and think about how you are really doing in each area. Be honest with yourself. You may feel great emotionally and socially but physically your body is run-down and you're always exhausted. You may love your work and feel intellectually stimulated, but have no close girlfriends. Just like a bent or broken spoke on a wheel throws the whole wheel off kilter and won't carry the load for long, if one or more areas of your life are not receiving enough attention, your life will be off-balance and your responsibilities will become nearly impossible to bear.

Instead of thinking about balance as a perfectly balanced scale, envision a tightrope walker that is continually adjusting to maintain her balance.

Sometimes we waver off-balance, rarely do we stand still, and there's a huge safety net of God, family, and friends to hold us and support us. So, the trick isn't so much in always "staying" balanced, but in being aware of the spokes on your life wheel and continually adjusting to return to balance over and over again. The benefits of being balanced are more satisfaction and joy inside our homes, our work places, and ourselves. We'll talk more about balancing your life later in the book. For now, it's important to do some soul-searching about your highest priorities.

Our vision and mission gives us conviction and direction. Without a vision, we lose sight of where we're going. Like a traveler without a map, we can easily get lost. A Momager with a strong vision has passion and purpose, and therefore can move mountains. This creates a tremendous amount of momentum that builds until the vision is accomplished.

Determining your vision, clarifying your values, and establishing your priorities will set you on a course for success. As you are bombarded with 100 things all at the same time, you'll be able to plan, prioritize, and do what's really important. If you know where you are going, you'll probably get there. Imagine that!

Chapter 4

I – Influential Communication.

Leaders Are Influential Communicators!

*"So I say, don't hold back. Don't be shy. Step forward
in every way you can to plan boldly, to speak clearly,
to offer the leadership which the world needs."*
-Claudia "Lady Bird" Johnson

A six-year old boy was telling his mother about an incident that happened at school that day. He concluded his story by saying, "I'd never do that!" His mother responded, "Never say never, because you never know when you might change your mind about something." Her son replied, "Mom, you just said never, three times." "Yeah, you're right," she said, "I should never say that again."

Sometimes, we say things that we don't mean. Sometimes we don't say things that we do mean. And sometimes, we don't say anything at all. Yet, in each scenario, we are communicating. We are always communicating. Whether we say one word, or not, we are always sending and receiving messages.

I have to thank my mother for giving me the "gift of gab." She can get people to open up and share their resources, ideas and most intimate thoughts with her.

As a Momager, it's critical to be a clear and strong communicator. That means not only being effective at sharing facts and figures, but really getting your family to understand you and striving to understand them. "A common theme present in most discussions of leadership for the 21st century is the leader's ability to create, articulate, and communicate, not only a vision, but more importantly, a global vision." These words by Karin Klenke highlight how vital good communication is to a leader.

Let me share this story about how I bungled communicating in a global way. While at a business meeting in London, a lovely, well-appointed British woman asked, "Where's the toilet?" What? Did she say *toilet*? She didn't say toilet, did she? How rude of her to call a restroom, a toilet. Aren't the English supposed to be proper and discreet? What seemed like a straightforward question brought up an array of judgements and assumptions. Instead of politely answering her question, I was confused and put off. What I didn't know at the time was that the British call the restroom the toilet. See how simple misunderstandings happen when we're communicating?

We think we're clearly asking a question and yet, how we ask it, what words we use, and the cultural context of the message all have an influence on how the message is received. Whether we speak the same language or not, communication differences are everywhere.

According to Theodore Roosevelt, "The most important single ingredient in the formula of success is knowing how to get along with people." I truly believe this. How well you can communicate determines how well you get along with others. Sounds easy, huh? Well, anyone who's raising a family or working with others outside the home knows that one of the biggest challenges of work and home life is getting along. One of my clients in human resources says, "We hire employees, but end up with people." People are only human. To err is human. A leader's role is to make sure people communicate and get along in a positive way, sometimes in spite of themselves.

We have the opportunity to learn new ways of communicating. It takes a conscious effort to learn and apply personal communication skills and an openness to receive honest feedback. You will get through to others more often if you apply the following techniques. Learn and practice the techniques, use them consistently, and your communication will become more authentic and clear.

The most crucial of all forms of communication is face-to-face. In this amazing time of technology, I've seen a disturbing trend among leaders to hide behind e-mails, letters, and the written word. I'm also seeing a real weakness among leaders in the art of persuasive communication. When we communicate in person, we are selling our ideas, our products, and ourselves.

Good communication builds a bridge of understanding between people. Good communicators make the complex seem simple and clear. They build people up.

Poor communication acts like a series of roadblocks, detours, or wrong turns down one-way streets. (Not a good idea, especially when there's a police officer waiting. Yes, I've been there and done that, in Italy, no less.) Poor communicators make concepts complicated and consequently, people feel frustrated that they don't know what's going on or what's expected of them. Poor communication wastes an awful lot of time and subsequently, money.

The key to any leader's success is his or her ability to communicate in an influential way. Laurie Beth Jones, author of *Jesus, CEO* says, "Leaders identify, articulate, and summarize concepts that motivate others. Most important, they boil concepts down to an understandable idea. Leaders have to see a situation from many levels, so they need to be open, approachable, and good at reading between the lines. Leaders have the added challenge of making the complex seem simple. Speaking with clarity and connecting to others are the hallmarks of good communicators."

If you're like most people, you fall between two extremes. Some things are easy to communicate, like good news and interesting information. The more difficult aspects of communicating include sharing bad news and dealing with conflict and discipline. An effective leader knows how to communicate face-to-face in all circumstances.

This chapter explores the connection between communicating effectively and empowering others to success. The three main topics we'll explore are: listening skills, non-verbal communication, and oral and written communication.

This communication definition by Robert Greenleaf, author of *The Servant Leader*, is a great way to begin our discussion. "Communication is the process by which the ideas, attitudes, convictions, and insights that help a group reach its goals come to operate through the right people at the right time."

This definition of communication has three major points.

1. Communication is a process.
2. Communication has a purpose.
3. Communication is done with the right people at the right time.

A small part of the total communication process is speaking or writing. And yet, what do we learn? Public speaking and writing. Listening is often overlooked and yet it is critical to our success.

Communication is a Process

Leaders sell their ideas, not just tell them!

One-way communication is when you tell someone something, but don't stick around to confirm if the other person has heard or understood you. Did you know when you speak only 35 percent of that message is retained? If we expect people to do what we want simply by just telling them once, we need to think again. Incorporating quality feedback and asking the other person to re-phrase what you said are very important.

Effective communication is a two-way process between the sender and the receiver. Like two people dancing, the sender transmits a message to the receiver and gets feedback. The receiver sends a message back and gets feedback from the sender. We send and receive messages verbally and non-verbally with our facial expressions and body language.

Communication Model

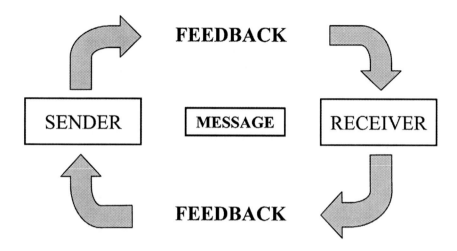

The following are required for two-way communication to work:

- The message must be clear.
- The receiver must listen and understand it.
- The sender must be credible.
- The receiver must be ready, willing, and able to act on the message.

Communication Has a Purpose

There are many reasons for communicating. Be sure you know what the purpose is before you open up the conversation. Often, we waste time and energy because we don't know what we are trying to communicate.

Reasons for communicating:

- Exchange information, opinions, ideas, and feelings
- Get others to do what we want them to do
- Reach decisions
- Solve problems
- Resolve conflicts

- Provide feedback
- Influence others to act
- Reach understanding
- Plain old venting and seeking support. (I do this one really well.)

Communicate With the Right People at the Right Time

To lead and influence, we must first consider the question, "Who is the right person to deliver this message?" Ask yourself, who is the best person to share this message? Why? We usually don't give that much thought to this part of our communication. If we do, we'll recognize people will follow the lead of others who are similar to them. As leaders we need to "get over ourselves" and focus on what's best for everyone.

"Harnessing the Science of Persuasion," an article in *Harvard Business Review*, says we are social creatures and rely heavily on the people around us for cues on how to think, feel, and act. One experiment included a group of researchers who went door to door in Columbia, South Carolina, soliciting donations for a charity. They showed potential donors a list of neighbors who had already donated to the cause. The longer the donor list was, the more likely those solicited were to donate.

To the people being solicited, the friends and neighbors names on the list were a form of social evidence about how they should respond. As a Momager, you probably already know that this type of persuasion is used by parents, "Everyone will be wearing a suit, so you must wear one too," and by children, "All my friends are allowed to do it."

If you're trying to implement a new idea or rule within your family and it doesn't go anywhere, consider changing the messenger or how the message is presented. Peer influence is very powerful and should be used whenever possible. Based on the purpose of your communication, you may also need to alter the time and place the message will be delivered. Remember the adage, "There's a time for everything."

If you have a heated discussion on the horizon, make sure it's the right time and place. Schedule family meetings at times that are convenient for everyone. If someone is tired, hungry, or cranky, by all means, re-schedule. If you are overly emotional about an issue as a result of anger, fear, guilt, or any number of strong emotions, give yourself some time to cool down. Communicating with emotion is essential to being understood, but only if that emotion is under control. If we are out of control we actually lose much of our power because we are so distraught that we can lose our perspective. People buy on emotion and justify with fact.

When a conversation is not going well, we can just say, "This conversation is obviously not productive. Can we talk about it later?" Time-outs are not just for children. They're great for adults too and provide an acceptable way to cool off and compose yourself.

Send Clear & Concise Messages

What the heck are you talking about?

LeighAnn Fulford, Momager of three says, "Communication is key to everything in life." It's so easy to think you are being clear, but leave out the details. For example, telling a child you expect good behavior in the store isn't clear communication unless your child explicitly understands your definition of "good behavior." Instead, say, "When we are in the store, I expect you to stay beside me and you must not touch anything without my permission." I've been doing this with my youngest child and it really helps.

Have you ever had a conversation with someone and thought they knew what you were talking about, only to find out they had no idea what you were communicating? The following are five elements that will enable you to communicate clearly and productively.

Five Elements to Ensure Clear, Productive Dialogue

1. **Know what/why you want to communicate.** Be clear about what you want to accomplish.

If the sender is unclear about what he/she wants to say, the receiver has the challenge of filling in the gaps -- a difficult, if not impossible, task.

2. **Tailor your communication style to the receiver.** Know the listener's needs, personality style, and interests.

Aim the message to the experience level of the listener. Use the right communication method. Sometimes, the spoken word gets the job done. Other times, you may need to use written or visual means to produce better results. With selling, you always need to know what the benefits are for the other person to influence them to your way of thinking.

Think of Benefits on Three Levels

Individual benefits -- How will the new idea or rule benefit the other person?

More free time, money, fulfillment, sense of responsibility, fun?

Team benefits -- How will it benefit the team? Recognition, closer team spirit, increased empathy or respect?

Organization/Culture benefits -- How will it benefit the entire family, organization, or society? Less arguing and conflict, more cooperation, increased accountability? Frequently remind your family of the benefits in a supportive way. Connecting with your family members or team builds morale and a feeling of involvement and commitment.

3. **Establish your Credibility and Rapport**

We're more likely to pay attention to people we trust, like, or feel in harmony with. It has often been said, "People don't care how much you know until they know how much you care."

To generate rapport, find common experiences or interests that you can build on. Perhaps you share an interest in music, travel, bowling, or gardening. Try and make a personal connection. Passion also helps sell ideas. As Joan Lunden says, "Happiness and enthusiasm are powerfully attractive; they draw people to you and make you successful."

4. **KISS**

Keep It Simple Sweetie

Use language that's common and easy to understand. Be sure to speak to your children in language that is age appropriate. Really pay attention to the words you use and the effect they have on others. Are the words inclusive or pompous and exclusionary?(See how big those words are.) By watching someone's reaction as you talk to them, you can usually tell if they understand. Watch their facial expressions and read their body language. Tailor your message to the receiver. "We" is the most important word. Use I or We statements instead of You statements. This is one of my biggest pet peeves in communication. People say, "You think. . . and you are . ."

Whenever we begin with the word *you*, we are speaking for the other person and putting words in his or her mouth. Most times, we can not fully speak for another person or group. Even if you think you can speak on behalf of someone else, it's better to say, "I think you mean. . ." or "I believe you mean . . ."

Whether it's with family members, or with your children's teachers, using "we" brings people together. Identify what the core issue is you want to explore and then share your different angles or viewpoints. Here's an example from a parent teacher conference. "I want to discuss how we can help Susan with her organization skills." This opening line clarifies the teacher and I are on the same team and opens up ideas from both of our unique perspectives.

Don't Say:	Do Say:
You should . . .	I think you may want to consider . . .
You want to . . .	I hear you want to . . .
You feel elated about . . .	It sounds like you're excited . . .
You like . . .	We have that in common, I like . . .

"I or We" messages are facilitative. They explain the problem, our feelings, and the effects of others behavior on us. When we use "I or We" messages:

Communication remains open
Problems can get solved
We can create a win/win situation
We feel better about the situation and ourselves
We express ourselves more clearly and with less judgement
Frame statements so they are positive and consistent.

Negative	Positive
We can't do it that way	That's a creative angle
Don't hit your brother	Let's use gentle touches
No, we just can't . . .	There's two ways of looking at this
Why can't you just . . .	I want you to consider . . .

5. Make Sure Your Verbal and Non-verbal Messages are Consistent and Truthful

Let me ask you a question. When you communicate, what do you think is most important in terms of how the listener interprets and understands your message? Is it what you say, how you say it, or your body language and/or facial expression? Take a guess. The three percentages should add up to 100 percent.

_____% Words only - Verbal message

_____% Tone of voice and inflection - Vocal message

_____% Other non-verbal factors -Visual message (facial and body expressions)

I have asked thousands of people this question and most people rank words between 30 to 50 percent, tone of voice between 30 and 40 percent, and non-verbal communication between 5 and 25 percent. Most people are absolutely and positively misguided when it comes to how they can communicate effectively.

Here are the real results from a landmark study conducted by Albert Mehrabian of UCLA:

7 % Words
38 % Tone and inflection
55 % Other non-verbals

So you see, what you say and how you say it are very important to building bridges of understanding. Focus your attention on what your body language is conveying, the tone of your voice, and being consistent with all three elements. Follow the adage, "*Say what you mean and mean what you say.*" This is so critical because being consistent with our words and actions builds trust. If you say one thing and really don't mean it, you are being inconsistent and others can sense something is wrong. Has that ever happened to you? You know you are uncomfortable with someone, but you don't know exactly why? Your powers of observation usually decipher the truth.

Not being consistent creates mistrust and weakens your message. This doesn't mean you should say everything on your mind. When you do decide to speak up, make sure it is authentic, honest communication that is never cruel. Remember when Mom said, "Don't stoop to their level." I have seen so many people convey inconsistent messages. Quite often someone can say one thing but their gestures say something else, like when someone says yes, but shakes his head, no. Often, someone has a wonderful idea, but the tone they use to share the idea, or their body language, can send a mixed message. The adage "It's not what you say, but how you say it," rings so true. This inconsistency is probably the biggest factor to ineffective communication.

I advise clients, *"Don't say anything, unless it improves on silence."* If we would just slow down enough to think before we speak, our communication would be much more powerful. Remember "Silence is golden." When the time is right and you are armed with something valuable to say, speak up. Don't be afraid to be loud and clear when you decide to speak. And by all means, make sure your tone and expressions match your words.

Non-verbal Behaviors Can Strengthen or Weaken Your Message

Solid Eye Gaze: Looking sincerely and steadily at another person.

Every mother has it as her secret weapon. It's called "The Mommy Look." Do you know what I mean? The look that conveys a child is doing something wrong. You can see it in church. Moms have this amazing ability to stare at their children (usually eyes are bulging and nostrils are flaring) and children know they need to behave. Moms also develop a loving gaze that is reserved only for their children when they do something especially well. The pride and joy radiates from Moms when they are happy with their kids.

The eyes have been referred to as the windows to the soul because they reflect what's happening within us. Holding a gaze for three to five seconds is normal (whatever "normal" means!). Maintaining eye contact for more than ten seconds is generally reserved for intimate relationships. With others, it can become uncomfortable and be intimidating. Look into your family members' eyes and be interested in what they are saying.

Dress & Appearance: Dress, groom and appear appropriate for the environment.

Okay, so if that means dribble-proof blouses and half-inch heels for a while, you need to do whatever works. The *Wall Street Journal* highlighted what "Undercover Mom" (executive mother gone incognito) wears in the office.

- Turtlenecks and twin sets (no buttons allowed)
- Pants with elastic waist (for quick changes)
- Loose jacket (washable, so no trips to the dry cleaners)
- Low heeled boots (forget stockings, step right onto the soccer field)

Avoid:
- High heels (not good for chasing)
- Short skirts (are you kidding?)
- Silk blouses (just not dribble, dirt, or tug-proof)

Successful Momagers change their clothes so they can "fit in" to whatever environment we're in. And sometimes that means changing three or four times a day. Yes, we're flexible!

Voice: Use your voice as a rich, strong instrument.

Speak loudly, deeply, and clearly. Use the "roller-coaster" technique. Lift your voice and then let it plummet. A monotone voice is boring with a capital B. Women in business diminish their status if they giggle, speak in high-pitched voices or smile too much. The same is true when you're talking to your children. If you don't behave as if you're serious, they won't take you seriously.

Posture: Stand tall and move in a relaxed and natural way.

"Stand up straight," Mom reminded you. Keep your energy and enthusiasm moving forward. Relax and smile. Leaders, including Momagers, take up more physical space than subordinates. Extend your hands and arms over the back of a chair while sitting. Let your body grow in stature, not shrink down. Many women shrug their shoulders, cross their legs and arms, and you can literally see their body taking up as little room as possible. Expand your body into space and take up more room.

Personal Space: Respect others' personal space.

In America, within two feet proximity is considered an intimate zone reserved for close friends or family. Our personal zone – from two to four feet -- is reserved for high trust relationships. Our social zone is four to twelve feet. A leader's zone begins in the social zone and moves to the personal zone as trust builds. An instant check for the level of trust in a relationship is to get closer or move further away and see how people adjust their space accordingly. When talking to your kids, use their names, get their attention and get in close so you can understand each other better.

Communication Dance: Fitting in

To influence others, you want to relate to them. The mirroring technique helps you do this. Imagine you're a mirror and are reflecting the other person's gestures, rate of speech, and facial expressions. Copy the other person's body positions and gestures. Good communication is very much like a dance. One person takes a step forward, one back. If you adopt someone's posture and behaviors, you may find him or her coming around more readily to your way of thinking. Don't overdo it. Sometimes, differences impress people too. The dance continues until both people are exhausted or invigorated. Read your family members' expressions and be aware of your gestures. Remember the amazing statistic that 93 percent of what we are expressing is based on non-verbal communication! Our interactions with others can be greatly improved if we notice and employ these key non-verbal signs.

Listen Lavishly

Why do you think we were created with two ears and only one mouth? Maybe because we should spend twice as much time "listening lavishly" as we spend speaking.

When good listening occurs, you communicate to others that:

• You hear and understand them.

• You care about and accept the speaker as a person.

• You appreciate the feelings that underlie their words.

• They can fully express their thoughts and ideas without judgement.

Leaders Know the Value of Being Lavish Listeners. James Biggar, CEO of Nestle Enterprises, said, "The fine art of listening is surely more important than talking. Often we fail to realize we can't hear when our mouth is moving. In life, leaders must always provide a channel for open feedback. The failure to listen means a refusal to change." Lavish listeners pay attention, and give feedback both verbally and non-verbally that tells the speaker, "I hear you."

Lavish Listening takes time. Make an investment of time in the people who are important to you. Team members, family members, and all the people within your circle of influence need to get enough time and not feel rushed when they speak to you. A wise mother once told me, "When your children come to you, stop what you're doing and listen." As leaders, when others come to us we need to be available. If we're not, opportunities to support, problem solve, advise, or lead may pass by quickly. If you can't speak with them immediately, be sure and schedule a meeting time. Most Momagers agree they need to be proactive and schedule time with all their family members weekly, if not daily. Slow down. Invest the time in your family with good-quality listening.

Don't Be a Lame Listener

I believe there are a whole lot of "lame listeners" in America today. Lame listeners pretend they're listening, but they're not. Lame listeners are thinking about other things while you're talking. Usually what they are going to say back to you. Or they're busy judging whether what you're saying is right or wrong. "Do I agree or disagree?" They're drawing conclusions about you and assuming they know what you are going to say. Lame listeners judge people before they have all the facts.

One story comes to mind about a lame listener. And believe you me, there's more where this came from. I was working with a non-profit arts organization in England that was approximately 25 miles outside of London. We were having a strategic planning brainstorming session discussing how we could attract more patrons to the center. They had the challenge of being so close to London and the amazing theatre district that is located there.

The brainstorming session began with the rules of good brainstorming:

- No idea is a bad idea
- Generate a high quantity of ideas
- No idea is to be judged for "practicality"

Although the rule is that no idea is to be judged, one of the team members seemed only able to follow this rule "verbally," meaning she didn't actually *say* anything negative. However, she disrupted and ruined the session with her nonverbal communication. She made faces, huffed, and rolled her eyes.

Many other brainstorming sessions have been highly successful, and brainstorming is a fantastic way for your family to cooperatively solve problems, plan the next family vacation, and come up with new ways to keep the house clean.

Did you know we can think about four times faster per minute than we can speak? It's no wonder our minds wander while listening to others. Sometimes we fill the gap by making judgements. It's important to avoid pre-judging and jumping to conclusions. Making judgements or self-imposed mandates are ineffective because they are usually one-sided. They lay blame on the other person you're talking to as if their behavior is the sole cause of the problem.

Words can lift others up or tear them down. Choose your words wisely because they will determine the outcome of your encounter. Avoid sloppy and foul language. This may seem obvious, but I hear an awful lot of swearing. Even if everyone else is doing it, it's harmful to relationships. The foolproof test as for whether you should say something or not is whether you would mind hearing your words repeated. Our followers, whether they have three-year-old ears or 30-year-old ears, are always listening to us and are ready to repeat our words and follow our examples.

Tips to Build a Bridge of Understanding

Focus on the behavior. Instead of saying, "Don't you have any pride in your things, pick up this pigsty." Say, "I expect your room to be 'clutter free' by the end of the day." If it's not, we will take away all the clothes left on the floor and you'll have to earn them back. Use specific situations and consequences to support your concepts. Separate the person's attitude from the behavior. This is tough, but amazingly effective. Always try to retain the person's integrity and stick to the facts. Let others know they are valuable but the behavior needs to change.

When resolving a conflict between two people, get them both on equal footing. Sit down together and be sure you're eye to eye. Acknowledge both person's position. There are always two sides to every story. Find out what both sides look like. To be a lavish listener, you must put yourself in the other person's frame of reference. Give quality feedback and be a skillful questioner.

Responses to Show You're Really Listening

We use both verbal and non-verbal factors when we speak and listen. Effective non-verbal listening usually includes head nods like a bobbing dog head, eye-contact, various non-words like "hhmmmm" or "Uh huh." These factors tell the other person you are paying attention, are interested, understand, and are involved in the conversation. Ask questions and offer supportive comments. Make sure you understand the facts and underlying feelings of the message.

There are four basic responses to validate you've heard the other person. They are reflecting, probing, advising, and supporting.

• **Reflecting:** Making a response to the speaker that reflects to verify what he/she is saying.

- **Probing:** Looking for more information or clarity. Most probes are in the form of questions.
- **Supporting:** Making statements that show empathy or understanding for the other person's situation.
- **Advising:** Providing new information to reinforce or change the other person's idea.

Here's an example of each response:

"I'm just not going to put up with him anymore!"

Reflecting:	Sounds like you're fed up with him.
Probing:	Tell me, what problems are you having with him?
Supporting:	(empathize) It sounds like you've had it. Are you exhausted working with him?
Advising:	Why don't you just knock his block off? (Only kidding! Thanks Lucy.)

"Mom, I want to go to the mall."

Reflecting:	So, you would like to go to the mall.
Probing:	What do you want to do at the mall?
Supporting:	Oh, I just love the mall too.
Advising:	Are you asking if you can go the mall? Because you know, we ask first in our family.

You can practice reflecting responses by using a variation of the "echo technique." You know how an echo works. One person says something and the echo repeats it back. For instance, if you yell at the top of your lungs, "You're a super person" the echo replies "You're a super person." (Try that some time; it feels really good) To use the echo technique, you rephrase what they said with a few minor changes.

Do	Don't
"Did I hear you say . . . ?"	Just walk away and assume you get it
"So what you really want me do it."	"You know what to do; go to do is . . ."
"Do you want me to do x or y?"	"Surely you understand by now."

When we echo back to others, we are confirming that we understand what was said and what needs to happen next. Most people initially think this is too repetitive. However, after they do it for a while, they discover how many times they misunderstood and how much time they save when they understand and get it right the first time.

Don't Ever Do This!

Sometimes people preface a question with an apology. This is especially prevalent among women and college-age girls. They say, "I don't know if this is what you're looking for but . . . ." or "This is probably wrong but . . ." Don't do this! Ever. You lose your credibility and confidence when you follow this approach. Don't apologize for your thoughts and ideas. Speak up with a confident, strong voice or exercise some of those wonderful listening skills.

Every time you communicate, you can either build up or tear down the relationship. Choosing to build each other up brings cooperation and creates positive relationships. The goal is to have an open, honest environment in the home where children feel safe to talk to you about anything and anyone.

Lavish Listeners Pay Attention

Paying attention sounds so simple but how many of us really do it? I mean giving the other person our *full and undivided* attention. If we're really listening, we don't do anything else at the same time like working on our computer, reading the paper, filing, cooking, or keeping one eye on the television. You know what I mean, after we've heard the fifth "Maaaaaaaa," we want to tune them out but they just keep getting louder!

With the age of multi-tasking comes a reduction in quality communication. How about trying to give others your undivided attention for just one day and see what happens? I think you'll be amazed at how much more effective you are.

Frances Hesselbeing, editor-in-chief of *Leader to Leader* magazine, said her grandmother, Mama Wicks, was the person who had the greatest impact on her life and work. Why? Because she taught her the essential element of effective leadership -- the importance of listening. "When people are speaking, it requires they have our undivided attention. We listen to the spoken words and the unspoken messages. This means looking directly at the person, eyes connected -- forgetting that we have a watch, just focusing for that moment on that person. It's called respect. It's called appreciation. It's called anticipation -- and it's called leadership."

No "Buts" About It

When you use the word "but," everything you said before the "but" is disregarded. For instance, "Judy, you're one of our best performers, but you could still improve." Which is it? Is she a great performer, or does she need to improve. According to her manager, both of these statements are true. So, don't use them in the same sentence. Remember the timing issue. Instead say, "Judy, you're one of our best performers because you. . ." (list specific examples). Bring up the continuous improvement issue at another time. We need to give consistent messages when we speak and "but" creates an inconsistency.

Frances writes, "How many times has someone told us how well we have performed -- and we were feeling good about the feedback, listening carefully -- then we have heard 'but' and the positive, energizing part of the feedback was lost in the 'but' and what followed it. 'But' is nobody's friend -- listener or speaker. 'And' provides the graceful transition, the non-threatening bridge to mutual appreciation, the communication that builds effective relationships. Replacing 'but' with 'and' is the advice I could give to the leader who listens and wants others to listen with an open mind."

Some people are visual learners and no matter how much we speak, writing it down suddenly, amazingly, gets through to them. I'm a visual learner and people who work with me know they need to write things down, draw pictures, flow-charts, pie-charts, and graphs so I can clearly comprehend. If you've explained a procedure once or twice and the person still doesn't get it, use writing as a reminder or follow-up tool.

Get creative and stick post-it notes on bathroom mirrors, or bedroom lamps. You can put reminders on the TV that say: Remember to do homework before watching one hour of TV. Of course, notes in the lunch box are great reminders and also great ways to thank and praise your kids.

Most people need to hear something three times before it sinks in. So we need to get more creative about how we communicate if we want better results. I'm always surprised to hear people say, "I told him how to do this three times and he still didn't do it right." When asked if they followed up the procedure in writing, most times the leader didn't even think about it. The responsibility is on the leader to make sure others understand and comprehend. Remember, "Don't tell. Soft sell."

What you should and shouldn't say to your child

Parents magazine (June 2004) highlights the 9 things you should not say to your child and the five things you should.

Nine Things You Shouldn't Say To Your Child

1. Leave me alone. Don't bother me. I'm busy.
2. You're so . . . labels create a self fulfilling prophecy.
3. Don't cry. Don't be sad. Don't be a baby.
4. Why can't you be more like your sister/brother.
5. You know better than that or I can't believe you did that.
6. Stop or I'll give you something to cry about.
7. Wait till Daddy gets home.
8. Hurry up!

9. Great job or good girl/boy. Vague praise is meaningless.

Five things you should say to your child

1. Please and Thank you.
2. The rule is . . .make your expectations clear.
3. I forgive you.
4. I'm sorry. Don't apologize for being the leader and having to enforce rules. Apologize for something you did wrong.
5. I love you. Show them with words and actions ie; tousling hair, high 5's, thumbs up, etc.

Many women are powerful and effective and lead others by the force of their presence and their communication skills. Look at Governor Christie Whitman, Margaret Thatcher, Mother Theresa, Golda Meir, Barbara Dole, and Senator Diane Feinsten. Watch them on TV and see just how expertly they apply the skills we've talked about. You may be thinking "Hey, those are leaders and I'm not really like them." I know I did. Whether you're like them or not, the same communication skills will bring you success.

Communicating is a lifetime process. No one is ever a 100 percent excellent communicator all the time. We always find new habits that pop up, sometimes good, and sometimes bad. One thing is for sure, interpersonal communication is a multitude of skills. You can continue to learn, practice, and fine-tune your approach. You are well on your way. Enjoy the rewards of connecting with and understanding others in a deeper and more fulfilling way.

Communication Assessment

4-Always   3-Often   2-Sometimes   1-Never
1)   I communicate the right message at the right time.
                1   2   3   4
2)   I give careful thought about a message before I communicate.
                1   2   3   4

3)   I speak confidently and project self-confidence.

    1   2   3   4

4)   I think about who the best messenger is before I communicate.

    1   2   3   4

5)   I welcome feedback about my communication.

    1   2   3   4

6)   I try to exclude judging and personal prejudice.

    1   2   3   4

7)   I listen intently and check that I have understood before I reply.

    1   2   3   4

8)   I give my full, undivided attention when listening.

    1   2   3   4

9)   I am positive and civil when I meet others.

    1   2   3   4

10)   I take time to give people the information they need and want.

    1   2   3   4

11)   I use written briefs that give all pertinent information on a task.

    1   2   3   4

12)   I communicate via electronic media when it's appropriate.

    1   2   3   4

13)   I question others to find out what they think and how they are progressing.

    1   2   3   4

14)   I take notes for minutes, interviews, and research.

    1   2   3   4

15)   I apply the rules of good writing.

    1   2   3   4

16)   I test important letters and documents on reliable critics.

    1   2   3   4

17)   I take an active role in learning new communication techniques.

    1   2   3   4

18)   I make my reports accurate, concise, clear, and well structured.
                1   2   3   4
19)   I apply the rule of soft selling to put across my points of view.
                1   2   3   4
20)   I understand how my audience will react to my communication.
                1   2   3   4
21)   I enter negotiations fully primed on issues and on the other side's needs.
                1   2   3   4
22)   I know the benefits for the other person to follow.
                1   2   3   4
23)   I respond positively to feedback from employees and others.
                1   2   3   4
24)   I am comfortable about asking others to do things for me.
                1   2   3   4
25)   I am comfortable expressing disagreement with issues in a constructive manner.
                1   2   3   4
26)   I can resolve conflict calmly and retain the other person's dignity.
                1   2   3   4
27)   I respond constructively when I receive negative feedback.
                1   2   3   4
28)   I give priority to communicating regularly with others.
                1   2   3   4
29)   I enjoy sitting and talking with my team/family.
                1   2   3   4

Results

    If you scored between:
    29-58
    You are not communicating effectively or enough. Listen to feedback and learn from your mistakes. Think about how you

can improve your communication skills through research, job shadowing, training, or coaching, and follow through.

59-86

Your communication is pretty good. Focus on improving your weak areas.

87-116

You communicate extremely well. Remember, your success as a leader relies on continuous listening and feedback. Keep up the great work!

I have a challenge for you. First, take some time and assess your communication skills. Look at an area of life you want to communicate confidently in and set one goal to ensure progress. Just start with one baby-step goal. Begin adding the elements you need to work on, one skill at a time. The time and efforts you invest will bring you the payoffs of more open and honest relationships and increased family and team synergy.

Chapter 5

C - Constant Change. Change, Change Go Away, Come Again Another Day

*"None of us knows what the next change is going to be,
what unexpected opportunity is just around the corner,
waiting to change all the tenor of our lives."*
- Kathleen Norris, Spiritual Writer, Best selling author

Remember singing, *"Rain, rain go away, come again another day?"* As children, we knew rain had to fall to nourish the earth and help life grow. It was just that we didn't want it to interrupt our life *today*. Isn't change just like that? Deep down we know (sometimes begrudgingly) that change is a natural and inevitable part of life. We even acknowledge that change can be for the best, but does it really have to affect our lives *today* and every day?

Life is fraught with change. Just as the earth passes through seasons, so too, our families and lives must change. Our kids change and go through so many different stages. In our families, there are changes through marriage, blended families, divorce, death, new births, moving, and of course...aging. There are so many physical changes as we age. My husband says, "I feel like I've been married to three different women (just me) since we've been married." I tell him, "Fasten your seatbelt and hold on baby, because it will feel like ten different women by our golden anniversary!" Why are botox and other body-enhancing procedures so popular? We're trying to look young on the surface. As a nation, we invest millions of dollars each year in a battle to resist the changes that go hand-in-hand with physical aging.

We also experience economic changes throughout our lives. Whether we have more money or less, each change brings different challenges. In addition, we are affected by social changes that alter how we exist and influence what we think is right or wrong.

The point is, change is with us. Now and forever. No wiggling our way out of this one. Wouldn't it be great to be able to wave a magic wand and make life stand still sometimes? Well, that's just not reality. The old adage is "the only constant is change." Accepting that change will always exist leads us to the next burning questions. How do we manage the changes as they occur? And, when we know that a change is necessary and will be good for our family, how do we create that change?

We can look to music for the answer. What does a band conductor do to make beautiful music and great formations on the field during half time? What is an orchestra director doing during a symphony? They lead the whole band with all the various instruments and sections. They take levels of ability into account and blend them to make a concert or symphony. Each instrument has a different sound and role to play. To get the band in tune and in step, each person's part is clearly identified. Everyone knows his or her part and executes it with precision so that all the pieces fit together. The flute doesn't say to the drum, "I wish I sounded more like you." The flute knows it has a unique sound and special time to perform and shine.

None of the instruments are competing with each other. Rather, they are harmonizing. They change beat, tempo, and pitch, all the while blending together to create a unified sound. The constant variation and changes in a piece of music are what make it so interesting and beautiful. The orchestra director is focused on the integration of all the pieces to create the best concert. The band major has the vision of the whole piece, while directing each musician according to his or her special talents. The wind instrument director is focused on his section of the piece and ensures his group blends together and feeds into the larger vision of the musical piece.

To lead your family to produce beautiful music, the same principles apply. Great leaders keep the vision and purpose of the whole song and enable every team member to connect to it in their own unique way. They recognize that the people and the instruments are changing constantly. They also recognize that the team's strength is largely the result of its diversity. In other words, each instrument is different, and therefore operates differently, sounds differently, and supports the band or orchestra in a different way.

Strong leaders know that their team members are all different and value those differences. Sometimes, however, leaders act like they want to make a team of clones. If you think that would be conflict-free, think again. If everyone were the same, you would have total boredom and stagnation. Your family is, in a sense, a team of diverse individuals who can stimulate new ideas and create a synergy that can continually thrive throughout all of your lives.

Key Elements To Creating a More Cohesive Family Team
- Ask each family member to share his or her strengths, interests, and passions.
- Include all members and build your team around the strengths of each person's contribution.
- Encourage and stretch each other to reach goals.
- Deal effectively with conflict and problem solving.

"Change, Grow, and Stretch to New Heights!"
- Me
"Learning how to respond to and master the process of change -- and eventually excel at it -- is a critical leadership skill for the 21st century. Constant, rapid change is a fact of life for all of us," comments Jennifer James, PHD, cultural anthropologist and author of seven books.

How do you create a learning environment?

John Mack Carter, as Editor–in–Chief of *Good Housekeeping* said "We all know that learning is a journey that never ends." Fostering a learning attitude and culture are hallmarks of effective leaders and parents.

If you want to become an agent of change and a person who makes a positive difference, the following tips provide a road map for you.

- ❑ Take full responsibility for yourself and your children. I know this can feel heavy at times.
- ❑ Model for your children what you expect from them. They do what you do, not what you say.
- ❑ Each family member takes ownership for his/her behavior and responsibilities.
- ❑ Hold the team accountable to each other.
- ❑ Let family members rely on each other and build team synergy.
- ❑ Don't blame others.
- ❑ Focus on problem solving instead of complaining, criticizing, and condemning.
- ❑ Motivate with challenging, yet achievable goals.
- ❑ Foster open communication among all family members.
- ❑ Let children share in the responsibility for leading sometimes.
- ❑ Think of each failure or mistake as an opportunity to learn.

Different Learning Styles

We all learn differently. Think about how you and everyone in your family learn so you can save time and frustration. Convey messages clearly by using appropriate learning styles.

Three Primary Styles of Learning

- Visual Learners -- Learn best by seeing the material. They retain information from notes, demonstrations, flash cards, charts, diagrams, forming pictures in their mind, and making use of color.
- Auditory Learners -- Learn best by hearing the information. They absorb information from lectures, discussions, TV, and music. Reviewing information out loud, and using memory tricks involving rhythm and rhyme are effective.

- <u>Kinesthetic Learners</u> -- Learn best by doing and experiencing. They most easily grasp information through role-playing, labs, and hands-on activities. They like to be able to move around while they work, and enjoy using tools and manipulating objects. Writing or typing their notes helps them to learn and remember what they've read or heard.

When you are sharing new information with your children, the more senses you involve and the wider variety of methods you use to teach or demonstrate, the better your children will understand and remember what they learned.

Education expert, William Glasser says, "Students learn:

10% of what they read,
20% of what they hear,
30% of what they see,
50% of what they see *and* hear,
70% of what is discussed with others,
80% of what they experience personally, and
95% of what they teach to someone else."

Momagers can use this information every day. Children can use this information to study and perform better.

Every Momager, and her family, will thrive if they have a learning environment. Establishing that your family operates in a "learning environment" means that each person agrees to learn something from everything that happens.

Connie Duckworth, Managing Director of Goldman, Sachs & Co. believes the four "F" words are important to success. "First of all, there's focus, flexibility, feedback, and failing forward, because you can learn just as much or more about what you want to do by doing some things you didn't want to do. I've had numerous situations like that, but from each area I've taken away a lesson that has served me and helped develop an array of experiences, and made me a better business person and a stronger person for it."

A Momager:

- Sets clear goals, objectives, and priorities
- Observes each child's performance and the family's behavior
- Provides timely feedback, both positive and corrective
- Recognizes and rewards winning performance

Set SMART Goals, Objectives, Priorities

*"Nothing changes until the pain of remaining the same
is greater than the pain of changing."*
Author unknown

To keep your family members focused on your family's vision and their individual objectives, set SMART goals. A goal is a statement of results to be achieved. Goals describe conditions that will exist when the desired outcome is achieved. We all know how to set goals on paper. How to achieve those goals is another story. Let's review how to set SMART goals, because they have a much better success rate.

- Specific-Be clear about what you want to achieve.
- Measurable -- Have a way to measure your success.
- Attainable -- Set goals that are challenging, yet achievable.
- Results oriented -- Envision what the results will look like.
- Timebound -- Determine what you will you achieve by what day/time.

Examples of SMART goals:

o Lose 10 pounds by Jan. 31. The scale and the calendar never lie!
o Complete writing the book by March 30.
o Win a gold medal at the regional track meet.
o Complete cleaning my bedroom by this Sunday.

When you set SMART goals for yourself and help your kids to set their own, you are held accountable to a measurement of result with a time and date. It's amazing how many work and personal goals never include the time frame. We have to be able to know when we have achieved success or initial failure of our goal. The only way you can hold yourself and others accountable are with goals.

Observe Performance and Behavior

What are you looking for in your children? If you're looking to find what they're doing wrong, you'll probably find more than enough information. If you're looking for what they're doing right and for their real strengths, you will find that too. Identifying each family member's strengths and the family's combined strengths will promote a much stronger sense of worth for each member.

To change or encourage change, we want to focus on behavior, because that is what we have the ability to alter. We need to look deeper and see what the person does/doesn't do that is the problem. Do they use rude language? Are they passive and not jumping in to help out when help is needed? Do they criticize others? Do they talk about people behind their backs? Always focus on behavior, not attitude. Work to change behavior.

The next stage is to identify the strength of the team. What is your family, as a team, really good at?

When a family member comes to you with a problem or a complaint, help them to envision what they would like to see changed. Ask your child if he or she is ready for some coaching. Before coaching, make sure your child is open to it. Ask questions to determine a child's interest in being coached. Use questions such as:

- Is now a good time to discuss this, or should we wait a little longer?
- Would you care to talk about what happened?
- When would be good to discuss this?

If your child is not immediately receptive, explain the benefits of the change. Don't ever insist on coaching when your child is not open for it. You'll do more harm than good and neither party will win. You know they aren't receptive if they get angry, defensive, or silent.

Don't coach if:

- You are angry or upset about the situation. Cool down first.
- You or the other person are very busy and now is just not a good time.

Provide Timely Feedback -- Both Positive and Corrective
Let's say all the conditions are right for coaching, the stars are finally aligned, and now you are going to give feedback. All feedback should be positive. Even if you're correcting someone, the feedback should be positive. Everything you say should be focussed on helping your child to perform better.

There are many ways to give feedback. Two processes that are extremely effective are:

- Meeting with an individual when you're trying to demonstrate how a task should be done.
- Giving positive/negative feedback. This is especially powerful when you're problem solving together.

Demonstrating a Task
Step 1 – Observe and analyze performance. This is done before meeting with the family member.

Step 2 – Create a relaxed atmosphere. Ask the person how they're doing. Inquire about their hobbies, school projects, or interests. Talk about anything that will help the person you are about to coach to feel more comfortable and relaxed. Give them positive reinforcement about something they have been doing particularly well.

Step 3 - Identify the area of performance that needs improvement. Ex: "Homework hasn't been done by 7:30 p.m. for the last three nights." After you give your observation of the issue, open the discussion about what is causing the problem. This is where listening is critical and using open-ended questions will result in a clear understanding of the problem.

Step 4 – Make suggestions for improvement. Demonstrate how the task should be performed and verify that they understand what they need to do differently.

Step 5 – When appropriate, have your family member demonstrate, and give him or her feedback on the performance.

Step 6 – Set up a follow-up time to review your child's progress and make alterations in the improvement if needed.

Sharing feedback, especially constructive criticism, is difficult for most of us. It can become more dangerous if we give wrongful criticism. Generalized praise also misses the mark. You want to use specific examples of behavior and demonstration in order to improve performance.

> *"We find comfort among those who agree with us–*
> *growth among those who don't."*
> Frank A. Clark

WISC Feedback Model for Change

This model helps you discuss a situation to gain involvement and commitment for improvement. If you're wise, you won't let good things go unnoticed and you won't let problems fester either. You will give timely feedback so your children know what they are doing well and what they need to improve on. Immediate feedback capitalizes on strengths in a timely way. This model helps you plan your feedback prior to discussing it. Here's how to whisk away poor behavior or give positive feedback with the WISC Feedback© technique:

Step 1 – W - What is currently happening?

Describe current behaviors that you want to reinforce through praise or redirect through constructive criticism to improve a situation.

Tips to Remember:

- Describe specific behaviors, not personal traits or habits.
- Avoid judgements, evaluations, or subjective language.
- Be open and available to discuss both sides of the story.
- Don't ramble on without seeking input or responses.
- Be brief. Keep it short and simple so the person doesn't become overwhelmed. Focus on only one or two points at a time.
- Present feedback at an appropriate time and place. Remember the teachable moment.

Step 2 - I - Impact

Describe the impact the behavior is having on others. Also mention the consequences of the impact. The more specific you can be in describing impacts, the more likely you will be to "sell" change. At this point, you are justifying your feedback. Answer the questions, "Why is this an issue we're focusing on?" "Why does the person need to change?" "What would happen if you didn't do anything and this behavior continued happening?"

Tips to Remember:

- Instead of being judgmental, be descriptive.
- Identify situations where the behavior affected other people, family members, neighbors, or the family as a team.
- Mention three or four effects and consequences.

Step 3 - S - Specific

Identify specific behavioral changes that will alter performance.

- Be creative as you generate alternative behaviors together.
- Be encouraging and offer ideas. Let your child retain responsibility for his or her current performance and commit to a plan the two of you create together.
- If your child doesn't have any ideas, offer a few ideas, but always preface them with, "I have a few ideas. Will they work for you?"

- When you reach an impasse, involve other family members in coming up with viable solutions.
- Address the issue in all its facets. There's almost always more than one way to improve a situation.
- Don't impose a solution from your perspective as the leader. Whenever you impose a solution, over-dependency may result. Your children lose the opportunity to think for themselves. People are not nearly as committed to an idea when it's not their own.

Step 4 - C - Constructive

Keep all feedback constructive. The goal of all feedback is to improve performance. It's not to vent your feelings and frustrations. It's not to criticize or condemn people for the way they are. Keep that in mind as you create a positive and encouraging approach.

Are We Having Fun Yet?

Focus on having fun while learning. You want to teach your children to play hard, no matter who the competition is. Playing to win means you want to beat your own individual and team goals. That can be lots of fun and exhilarating. Winning the game is also a goal but not the *only* goal. So, we need to put things in perspective and focus on growth and having fun. So many adults and parents take the fun out of playing by being so serious all the time. Try to create an atmosphere of playfulness in which your family appreciates the game, teamwork, and synergy.

Sandwich Feedback

All feedback should take into account the "sandwich philosophy." Like a sandwich, you have two pieces of bread and the filling. Sandwich all constructive feedback in between positive remarks. This way, you begin and end on a positive note.

For example: David, you get such good grades and know you want to do well in school. That's why I'm so surprised you haven't been studying for the past week.. Is something going on we could talk about?

I'm often asked, "Why do I have to give all this feedback?" Many people believe that kids are just supposed to listen and obey because that's what they're supposed to do. Well, times have changed. For people – including your kids -- to stay motivated, involved, and follow your lead, you need to give plenty of feedback.

Negotiate!

You can manage and change relationships with negotiating. A Momager has to be a great negotiator. Call it what you want. We've all heard the pleading, bargaining, coaxing, begging. Pleeeze, pleeeze, pleeeze Mom. can I go? Everyone will be there except me. Or. . .everyone else has it! C'mon, Mom." Negotiating with your partner and kids seems endless at times. The strain can be enormous unless you can negotiate like a pro.

Use Negotiating Skills To:

Navigate balancing chores (unless you do everything yourself, Yikes!)

Get "buy in" from your husband/partner about your game plan

- Decide who's going to do what and when
- Determine TV time, chore schedule, house rules, etc.
- Manage the kids' schedule. What activities will you and your kids participate in?
- Decide what school the children are going to and when they'll start
- Decide what the best discipline program is for each child. To determine who should discipline and when.
- Decide when and if the kids can have certain toys. (One of our best family negotiations was over when and how David would get a Play Station 2. Can you believe he ended up saving his money for a year to buy one? And, he was thrilled when he got it.)
- Determine how much your job and benefits are worth in the marketplace.
- Balance your work/home schedule - When will you stay home or go back to work?

Sibling Disputes and Your Role as Parent

Follow this three-step plan, so you can negotiate and stay in control.

Focus on a win-win outcome in which both people are satisfied. If both people can't be equally satisfied, make sure each person understands your position and why you hold this position.

1. Know your position. You must know what you want. Think about what you want out of the situation in the short-term and the long term. I'm convinced kids were born with the "bug you until I wear you down" negotiating tactic.

If your position is to not negotiate at all, then you need to communicate that up front. I like to say, "This is not negotiable." If you walk away and show you are not willing to discuss it, the other person gets the picture. I hear moms say, "Talk to the hand." When my kids would whine, they got to talk into the brown paper 'whine bag." Basically, I wasn't going to listen to it and they knew it. The discussion ends right there.

Now if you *do* want to negotiate, what do you want to get out of it? Set SMART goals about what your best case position would be and know what your "rock bottom" position is. (See the goal setting section for more information.) Differentiate what you *want* and what you *need* from the situation. Always determine these two positions so you can be flexible and ready to give and take. Decide what you are willing to give up and what you really want.

2. Know the other person's position. What does the other person want and need? Spend time truly understanding the other person's frame of mind and heart. Spend just as much time trying to understand their perspective.

3. Create a Win-Win Outcome. This involves both parties coming together and agreeing on a mutually beneficial outcome. There aren't winners and losers. You can usually give and take so both parties are winners. Sometimes this involves coming up with a third option that you hadn't previously thought of. When both

people win you have new perspectives and a greater appreciation of the other person's position

With a unified family team, a clear vision, SMART goals, and proven tools, you're all set to initiate real improvements in your family, neighborhood, and community. My most sincere hope is that you will embrace change and use it as an opportunity to re-think your values, beliefs, and ways of working and living. Change can give you tremendous power to recreate yourself, your family life, and the world.

Isn't it time to make some beautiful music? What would the world be like if we all created beautiful symphonies with our families? We could dance and sing and recreate our own little place on the planet. Start now. Today. Create your own beautiful symphony with the people around you. Go for it. The world needs your unique contribution!

Chapter 6

T-Teambuilding. Momagers Build Strong Teams

"Success is empty if you arrive at the finish line alone.
The best reward is to get there surrounded by winners.
The more winners you can bring with you
-the more gratifying the victory."
-- Howard Shultz

You and your partner are the head coaches of your team. To powerfully influence your team, you must be a coach of coaches, not a boss of bosses. In this chapter, you'll learn how to raise future leaders through creative coaching and feedback. "The objective in any team sport is to transform the group from a mere collection of talented individuals into a highly cohesive unit so that the whole is greater than the sum of its parts," said Colleen Hacker, sports psychology consultant to the U.S. Women's Soccer Team, winners of the 1999 World Cup Championship.

Now we have the challenge and opportunity of bringing the whole team together. Here's where the sparks really start to fly! If you want to raise responsible, loving children, the relationship between Mom and Dad serves as the foundation and example of love. At this point, partnership leadership is very successful. Mom and Dad have to show a united front and truly support each other. With this type of leadership you each have areas you are strong in and you share the responsibilities. A clear understanding of family hierarchy is key to making this type of partnership work.

The heads of the family are the parents, not the children. Dad is such a vital part of this partnership. He must listen to all the team members and at times make some very difficult choices based on what is best for the whole family. He has an obligation to listen to his wife and hear his children's opinions. In our family, Bob has the unique role as ultimate decision-maker because we follow a Christian model for our family. This is why it is vital for a woman to be a leader and share her perspectives.

In some families the woman is the ultimate decision maker, and in single parent family's – well – he or she is IT.

A Momager has precious and valuable information and her views must be given top priority. She has a strong opinion and shares it with a loving heart. She knows that sometimes "following" is a viable position.

We are starting with the assumption that effective teams have an environment based on commitment, trust, respect, and open communication. My son David had a fabulous basketball coach in fourth grade named Molly Horstman. She is also an executive with Johnson and Johnson and says she applies many of the same principles of coaching employees as coaching children. As Coach Molly says, "Commitment means never quitting; support for each other; belief in each other; trust; respect; *honest* communication."

The Four Main Aspects of Building a Cohesive Team

1   The Hallmarks of a Great Coach
2   How to really appreciate differences in people and teams.
3   Team roles every team must have.
4. How to energize and motivate your team with a *Motivational RAP©*: Recognition for their meaningful contribution, Accomplishments in their work, Participation in the decision making.

How We Can Use Coaching at Home and at Work

Did you know that even the best baseball players only hit about one-third of the balls they are pitched? More than two-thirds of the time, they strike out or someone catches the ball when they hit it. The batters appear to fail more than they succeed. Coaches realize failure is part of the game to reach peak performance.

Coaches used to seem like super-heroes. They were larger than life when I was a kid. I always wondered, "How do they get the teams to win? What did they talk about during half time?" Since I didn't play organized sports it seemed somewhat mysterious to me.

When two of my sisters played basketball in grade school and then in high school, I got to see good and poor coaches up close and personal. The veil was lifted. Throughout my consulting years, I have seen the amazing difference a great coach can make. I'll share with you what great coaches do and how you can be one.

Coaching has many definitions and the concept has moved from the athletic field into the education and business arena and now, with "Momaging," into the home. No matter where you apply the definition, the results are the same. Effective coaches produce winning teams. Winning is not always about winning the game as much as winning through people reaching their peak performance.

What is Coaching?

According to Webster's dictionary, coaching means "to train intensively by instruction, demonstration, and practice." You can only coach if you have a trusting relationship with the other person and the other person wants to be coached. You produce winning teams by working on people's strengths and learning from the failures.

- In business, coaching involves guiding employees to greater competence by increasing knowledge and sharpening skills and abilities.
- In sports, coaching focuses on developing stronger athletes and better scores.
- In education, coaching develops students who can reach their highest academic potential.
- In families, coaching guides children to reach their fullest potential in all aspects of their lives.

The goals of coaching are two-fold

I.   To provide direction for an individual

II To work together as a team to help each other find direction

To accomplish these goals everyone must take on greater responsibility and be accountable to the team for its performance. No one can really say, "That's not my job." Just as each family member's success depends on the family's success, the family's success depends on each individual's success. There is a high level of inter-dependency.

Intimidating Vs. Humble Coaches

There are many different styles of coaching. One style that is outdated is intimidation. Coaches who use intimidation lead by using fear. We've all seen coaches who yell and scream at the players from the sideline. Winning the game means everything to these coaches. When the game isn't going well, they look like they're going to "bust a gut." They become domineering and out of control. The intimidating leader thinks, "I am the leader and no one should doubt me or challenge my authority." There are too many of these types of leaders in existence.

How many of us have variations on this intimidating theme? Especially moms who are so tired of explaining instructions so many times. It's all too common to yell, snap, and then regret our words later. I've learned that we just can't take the hurtful words back once they spill forth from our mouths. Coaching relieves us of the burden of repeatedly explaining and puts the onus of responsibility on our children.

Everyone responds better to humble leadership. This is when the leader shows her strength, confidence, and vulnerability. The humble leader recognizes we're all human and that we all make mistakes. When she makes a mistake, she takes full responsibility, is the first one to apologize, and focuses on learning from the mistake and solving the problem. Coach Molly says, "The coach is not afraid to get his or her hands dirty or admit mistakes; yet remains very confident."

A Momager shares the challenges she faces with her family and lets them know she doesn't have all the answers. However, she is committed to the team and will go the extra mile. She is open in her communication and gives honest and timely feedback, whether it's good news or corrective.

Teamwork is the only way to succeed long-term. Teamwork is the process of working together to move an idea, goal, or situation forward. We all know that a team of diverse individuals has challenges. Differences in personality, gender, priorities, and goals can all present difficulties. That's why it's so important to have a strong vision and inclusivity. Let me clarify inclusivity because some people ask me, "Is being inclusive when you treat everyone the same?" No, this is not what the word really means. Everyone is different, so treating everyone the same is actually a form of discrimination. Effective leaders treat each person as he or she deserves to be treated based upon individual strengths, talents, and personalities. This approach is not always easy, but the payoff is immense.

How to Really Appreciate Differences

Coach Molly says " Diversity is key to a winning team! Differences create healthy internal competitiveness and challenge others to think differently and play differently. Diversity provides energy that must be managed."

The key is in managing diversity. There are so many ways to explore personality differences. I will share many options and you can decide which technique you want to implement with your family.

Team Roles

The Belbin Questionnaire designed in the U.K. gives a good overview of team roles. This indicator identifies eight types of people who contribute to making a crucial difference on team performance. They are:

- **Chairperson/Coordinator** - Coordinates the way the team moves toward group objectives.
- **Shaper** - Shapes the way in which team effort is channeled and sets objectives and priorities.
- **Plant** - Advances new ideas and strategies and pays special attention to major issues. They have a creative approach to problem-solving.
- **Resource/Investigator** - Explores and reports on new ideas and developments outside the team and creates external contacts. (I'm this type)
- **Monitor/Evaluator** - Analyzes problems, evaluates ideas and suggestions. Great with judgement and analysis.
- **Company Worker/Implementer** - Turns concepts and plans into practical working procedures. Has awesome organizing ability and practical common sense. (which isn't so common anymore).
- **Team Worker** - Supports team members in their strengths and builds on suggestions. Promotes team spirit and improves communication between members.
- **Finisher** -Checks details and ensures nothing has been overlooked. Maintains a sense of urgency and has powerful capacity to follow through.

This information can be helpful in many ways. It gives you an idea of how everyone is different so you can assign roles depending on your family's needs. Some members of your family might naturally fit one or more of these styles. And, thankfully, you don't need to have eight family members on your "team" to fill all the roles.

Say, for instance, that your family has difficulty finishing projects on time. A team with no finisher might have problems meeting a specific deadline. Allow an existing team member to modify his or her role in order to compensate for any omission in team make-up. You can appoint one person to formally focus on finishing each project or task. Give that person the authority to encourage and give positive or corrective feedback to the rest of the team for results, without any offense, of course. An example of the finisher playing his or her role might be they say to the team member: C'mon, let's try to finish folding the clothes in 15 minutes and then we can go out to play.

When working with teams, I sometimes adapt the concepts to just four types. When I go into organizations I can very quickly see who likes to do what and if they're well placed, or not.

The Four Primary Types

Idea Generators - Big picture people. Visionaries who generate new ideas and dreams. They look to the future and to other fields and come up with new opportunities for growth.

Implementers - People who take the ideas and mold them so they become a plan. Usually they're the team members that make it work in the real world.

Analyzers - Critical detail people who analyze and poke holes in the idea or product. They make sure the team goals are attainable and show where the weaknesses exist. They also focus on the finances so the project can be completed within the budget.

Organizers - Organize the team and the people so the project is finished on time. The organizers are the cheerleaders who focus on all the people so the goal can be reached with a high degree of team spirit.

Every team needs all these roles filled to be effective. There are no winners or losers on these teams. There are people with different natural gifts and you should select or assign roles accordingly.

Understanding Individual Strengths

Now let's turn toward understanding people in your family. There are many instruments to assess personality and behavioral types.

There's the Myerrs-Briggs Indicator, which has been very popular in America over the last 40 years and is based on Carl Jung's theory of personality types. It contains four scales: introversion-extroversion; sensing-intuition; thinking-feeling; and judging-perceptive. The Indicator is used mostly in personal counseling and coaching and sometimes as a selection instrument.

Other instruments to assess personality characteristics are the DiSC™ Personal Profile System and the Saville & Holdsworth's Occupational Personality Questionnaire (OPQ). If you and your family want to take a full assessment, there are many very good ones available. You can obtain them through a counselor, psychologist, trainer, or psychiatrist. The important thing is to understand yourself and your family members.

Understanding personality types enables you to:

- Identify consistent ways of behaving.
- Capitalize on strengths. Be aware of weaknesses.
- Increase your appreciation of different personality types.
- Communicate with others more effectively.
- Deal with potential conflicts with others.

Following, is a quick and easy reference to understanding different ways people behave. We can alter our behavior based on the environment, but we all have natural tendencies and those innate tendencies are what the assessment addresses.

Personality Assessment This tool will allow you to quickly evaluate someone's dominant style of behaving. Simply check the boxes that best describe the person's behavior. The style most often checked indicates the person's predominant behavioral tendencies.

Focus	"Bull"	"Monkey"	"Dog"	"Turtle"
Common Behaviors	❑ Clear, decisive, takes charge, blunt, positive	❑ Approachable, persuasive, misses deadlines, optimistic, enthusiastic	❑ Sincere, patient, actively listens, possessive, loyal	❑ Logical, precise, maintains systems, critical, careful
Work Station/Desk Appearance (if applicable)	❑ Stacks/piles, multiple projects, accomplishments displayed	❑ Colorful/creative, pictures of self with friends, designed to impress	❑ Personal belongings, family pictures, calm environment	❑ Impersonal, neat, graphs/charts on wall, efficient
Personal Appearance	❑ Bold, unusual, individualistic	❑ Stylish, trendy, flashy	❑ Comfortable, within policy guidelines, favorite clothes	❑ Conservative, well-groomed, blends in her policy
Favorite Subjects	❑ Business goals, personal goals, accomplishments	❑ Memberships, social accomplishments, themselves	❑ Family, trips, hobbies	❑ Details, processes, impersonal subjects
Favorite Comments	❑ *"Skip the details.."* *"What's bottom line?"*	❑ *"Let us, we, me..."* *"What's everybody doing?"*	❑ *"Let me think about it..."* *"How?"*	❑ *"This is not right..."* *"Why?"*
Walking Style	❑ Walks fast with purpose, carrying a project	❑ Stops to talk to people along the way	❑ Walks comfortably, smiling at everyone	❑ Walks while proofing a report
Listening Style	❑ Wants brief summary and will review details later	❑ Wants exchange of ideas/opinions and consensus building	❑ Wants time to digest information and consider others' opinions	❑ Wants proof of information and time to verify facts
Style Under Pressure	❑ Confrontational/ impatient, tighten control, distant	❑ Overly talkative, defensive, find the fun group	❑ Slow to change, stubborn, passive	❑ Perfectionist, formal, misses the big picture
Managing Style	❑ Direct, results-oriented, wants to skip details, quick	❑ Influences, sells ideas, team builder, inconsistent decision maker	❑ Honest, democratic, mediator, nonconfrontational with others	❑ Systematic, focused, organizes self/others, micro-manages
# Of ❑ Checked				

Identify what your style is and then identify your husband and children.

Can you see yourself and your family members more clearly now? It's amazing to discover how different we all really are. This knowledge can expand our horizons about other people and increase our sensitivity to how each of us is "wired differently."

Overview of the Four Different Styles

Bull -- Emphasis is on shaping the environment by overcoming opposition to accomplish results. A bull represents this person because they can be like a bull in a china shop.

My son Steven is this type and from a very young age I saw it. He was always moving. He would climb over *anything* -- sofas, balls, stairs, dressers – and any*one* to do what he wanted. He eventually overcame it. He can be very powerful when his energy is focused properly. In our family, Steven is like a fireball that is always trying new and different activities. He doesn't talk much, even grunts sometime, and makes quick decisions.

A Bull's Tendencies Include:

- A high level of confidence and a strong ego.
- Likes to generate ideas.
- Direct communication and quick decision-maker. Likes direct answers.
- Thrives on challenges and solving problems.
- Desires change.
- Questions the status quo and causes action.
  Each personality has strengths and weaknesses assigned to it. For the Bull to be more effective, this person needs:
- To understand they need people and recognize the needs of others.
- Weigh pros and cons more carefully, research facts, and calculate risks.
- Structure a more predictable environment.
- To pace himself or herself and to relax more. They're usually intense and driving.

- To identify with a group.
- Communicate reasons for their process and conclusions.

Monkey - Emphasis is on shaping the environment by influencing or persuading others. "Monkey See, Monkey Do" is this person's mantra. These people influence others to follow them or a cause.

A Monkey's Tendencies Include:

- Communicates in an articulate and persuasive way.
- Enjoys contacting people and participating in a group.
- Optimistic and enthusiastic.
- Makes a favorable impression.
- Creates a motivational environment.
- Establishes democratic relationships.

For the Monkey to be more effective, this person needs:

- Objectivity in decision making.
- Participatory management.
- Facts and a logical approach to decision making.
- Priorities and deadlines to stay on task.
- Direct communication.

Dog -- Emphasis is on cooperating with others to carry out the task. Much like Lassie or a seeing-eye dog, this person is supportive and loyal.

A Dog's Tendencies Include:

- Consistent at performing in a predictable manner.
- Loyal and patient.
- Interested in helping others.
- Good listeners who can calm excited people down.
- Maintainers of the status quo, unless given reasons for change.
- Wonderful at creating and maintaining stable, harmonious environments.

To be more effective, Dogs need to:

- React quicker to unexpected change.
- Obtain information on how their effort contributes to the total effort.
- Seek guidelines for accomplishing the task.
- Learn how to prioritize tasks.
- Be more flexible in their approach.

Turtle -- Emphasis is on working conscientiously within existing circumstances to ensure quality and accuracy. Like a turtle, this person likes to take their time and do everything systematically. "Slow and steady wins the race." Oftentimes, accountants and engineers are turtle personalities.

A Turtle's Natural Tendencies Are:

- Thinking analytically and logically, focusing on all the pros and cons.
- Concentrating on performance standards and procedures.
- Using a systematic approach to everything.
- Subtle or indirect approaches to conflict.
- Diplomacy with people.
- Critical, detailed. and careful.

For this person to be effective:

- Delegate important tasks.
- Use policies and procedures as guidelines, not written in stone.
- Initiate and facilitate discussions.
- Encourage teamwork and other people's opinions.
- Develop problem-solving techniques and tolerance for conflict.

You can see from all these differences, there are many areas where natural conflict arises. Look at the natural difference between a Turtle personality and a Monkey personality. They would have conflict about how they approach a project. The Monkey would be naturally optimistic and looking for how they could get people together to accomplish the goal. The Turtle would be detailing and analyzing the procedures and critically seeing where the mistakes are in the process. We need both types to get a project done well and it takes all our communication skills and conflict resolution techniques to work out the differences and truly understand each other.

Can you also see why all people are needed and can depend on each other to strengthen the team? Our family has five members and we represent every personality type. Thank goodness Tina Rose and I are the same type and we can totally understand each other without a lot of effort. By using this personality assessment tool, each family member can see what special gifts and strengths the others naturally bring to the table.

Darlene Duke is the mother of 12 children in Ohio. I interviewed her and this is what she had to say about different personalities and how she motivates them. "I have twelve different combinations of personalities that I have to address. Some respond with a simple word. Others test me to make sure I really want them to do something before they put the effort in to it. Because if they can get out of it, they will." Darlene spends time following up on tasks assigned. She doesn't just assign them and assume they will be done.

Creating and Motivating A Superior Team

"The best executive is the one who has sense enough to pick good men to do what he wants done, and self-restraint enough to keep from meddling with them while they do it." These words by Theodore Roosevelt speak volumes about team building. I really like the words "keep from meddling." Once we explain what has to be done, our job as a leader is one of motivating, recognizing, and follow-up. Not micro-managing!

Whenever I ask leaders what motivates people the most, the top three answers usually are:

1. Money
2. More money
3. Good Benefits

Nope these aren't the top three! The real top three answers are in the *Motivational RAP©*. C'mon sing along. . .

"You can energize your team with a *Motivational RAP©*."

Recognition and appreciation for their meaningful contribution, **A**ccomplishments and adding value with interesting work, and **P**articipation in decision-making. Let's explore how to motivate co-workers and kids to perform their best.

So, How Do You Motivate Your Children?

First, determine what motivates each one of your children. Just as each person has a different personality, each person has different motivating factors. I'll highlight many and you pick and choose based on your family members.

Recognition and Appreciation

"It's easy to complain about children. But when we want to express our joy, our love, the words elude us. The feelings are almost so sacred they defy speech."
- Joan McIntosh, Coach and Trainer

Darlene Duke shares these wise words about showing appreciation. "I find that motivation doesn't come with angry words or bossing. When I hear the kids get bossy, it irritates me and so I know it has to irritate them if I boss. I found that simple rewards are all it takes to get a job well done. If I assign a chore in the morning, then I ask that person when she or he will be done with the task. If they have done it well, I ask them if they would like to choose what we have for lunch or dinner. Or, maybe if they would like to come with me as a helper on an outing. Sometimes I will treat them to McDonalds. Sometimes they get to choose a movie the next time we watch one. My incentives are not costly and might seem ordinary, but they work with my family."

Here is a list of ideas to motivate through recognition and appreciation. Select the ones to use based on what each of your children would find most encouraging.

Personal Rewards

- Praise - Make it specific and show how it helps the family. Praise for a job well done and for effort. Don't praise too often though.
- Spread the good news. Tell everyone about better performance.
- Later bed time.
- Longer/additional breaks or playtime.
- Special privileges
- Gifts, awards, prizes (gift card from Toys-R-Us, or their favorite store, CDs, theatre tickets, sports events).
- Cards/memos of commendation. Handwritten letters are golden!
- Monetary/Tangible Rewards - A raise in allowance, payment for a task outside of a child's responsibility area, money deposited into a savings account or college fund.

"Look Ma, No Hands!" or "I Can Do It!" Approach to Accomplishing Goals

Kids and parents alike want to succeed and gain approval. You know how great you feel when you complete a big project that took a lot of hard work? There is nothing quite like knowing you are doing your best. Make sure the chores and goals your children have are interesting to them.

Here are some ideas for making work more fun and striving for goals more interesting.

- Praise for "job well done" when it's extra special. Not too much though.
- Special assignments with increased responsibility/authority
- Support for undesirable tasks
- Opportunities for advanced training/education
- Letters from leader or siblings highlighting how this member adds value.
- Teach other team members how to do tasks
- New responsibilities

- Delegated authority
- Celebrate success! Sometimes we're so busy thinking about the next thing that needs to be done that we forget to celebrate and thank everyone for their contribution. A Big Thank You encourages people to appreciate and relish their accomplishments.

Can I Help?

Participation is key to unlocking full potential.

Nothing motivates like being involved in one's own destiny. It has become apparent that the traditional authoritarian style of management is losing ground to participative systems which reward workers' input to the processes.

The flight of the human-powered Gossamer Albatross (plane) across the English Channel in 1979 is a remarkable feat of American technology. The Americans were competing against teams from Japan, England, and other European countries. The actual construction of the craft was accomplished under truly participative style.

In his book, *Gossamer Odyssey*, (Houghton Mifflin, Boston), Morton Grosser writes about how they produced such an incredible plane. The construction chief or foreman of the day, would go over to the airplane and write down all the jobs that needed to be accomplished. The list was usually written on yellow paper and posted on the hangar wall. Whenever someone finished what he was working on, he would look at the list and decide what he wanted to do next. People usually did what they were best at and they produced a successful plane in a remarkably short amount of time.

There is something we can all learn about this team participation approach. Sometimes you may find yourself involved in a project for which previous guideline are scarce. If you find yourself forced to start out in a new direction, these team lessons are extremely worthwhile.

Ideas to Increase Participation

Rotate Leadership

In the Gossamer project the posting of assignments were handled by one supervisor one day and perhaps another acting supervisor the next. Necessity and circumstances ruled how the team operated, not a prior agenda. The supervisors who became heavily involved in one phase of the project were relieved of overall responsibility by another member of the team. There was a net gain because of wider participation in various phases of the project.

Share the Responsibility

Each Gossamer member had to take a periodic look at what had been done and what needed to be done. This resulted in members who viewed the project in terms of its progress toward completion. They didn't just look at it from their own viewpoint. They looked at the project and thought about everything that had to be done.

Remember these wise words by Seneca, "No man can rule except one that can be ruled."

Allow Project Members To Choose Their Assignments

In the Gossamer project, the result of self-choosing jobs produced a sorting out of talent and personality that produced highly successful results. Much like in Harry Potter when each person puts on the "sorting hat" to determine which house he or she will be in. In our family, we have a stack of index cards with chores listed on them. The kids get to pick the chores and then trade them sometimes. The kids love the idea of choosing their chores. And I like not having to tell them what to do all the time.

Encourage Team Decision-making and Problem Solving

The synergy that happens with participation usually far outweighs the extra time. Participation is also an excellent motivator for people who complain about a situation. Let them be involved in problem solving and decision making and you'll be amazed at how quickly they turn around and take more responsibility.

With everything you've learned about visioning, influential communication, and team building, you are ready to transform your family team. Last, but not least, don't try to implement all these ideas at once! Take one or two of the ideas and slowly put them into play. As you and your family members begin to positively change you will see some new patterns. Morale will perk up. Commitment will build. Your children will begin to focus on solving problems instead of being defensive and territorial. Communication will be more honest and open. All this equals better relationships and improved results. The sky's the limit!

Coaching Survey

Rate your coaching effectiveness. For quality feedback ask your family members to rate you as well.

5 - Outstanding 4 - Very Good 3 - Okay 2 - Need improvement 1 - poor

1. I recognize differences in my family members and coach them accordingly.   5 4 3 2 1
2. I have a coaching/learning environment at all times.
                                                                5 4 3 2 1
3. I keep others informed about family plans and ways of operating.
                                                                5 4 3 2 1
4. I clearly define the job description and skills required to do the job
                                                                5 4 3 2 1
5. I define the ongoing expectations.
                                                                5 4 3 2 1
6. I encourage others to solve their own problems.
                                                                5 4 3 2 1
7. I give praise and other rewards to recognize achievement.
                                                                5 4 3 2 1
8. I keep everyone focused on team effectiveness and their own personal contributions.   5 4 3 2 1
9. Everyone on the team always knows the vision and goals.
                                                                5 4 3 2 1
10. I know the personal future aspirations of each member.
                                                                5 4 3 2 1

11. I look for ways to help people grow on the job.
5 4 3 2 1
12. I give immediate reinforcement for improvement or changes.
5 4 3 2 1
13. I ask team members to assist one another to learn and to grow.
5 4 3 2 1
14. I am available to the team and rate this as a high priority.
5 4 3 2 1
15. I encourage differing viewpoints.
5 4 3 2 1
16. I work hard to assure family members respect, support and understand each other.　5 4 3 2 1
17. I give high-quality, specific feedback.
5 4 3 2 1
18. I have a plan to develop each team member's skill or motivation
5 4 3 2 1

If you scored less than a four on any item, that is an area for personal improvement.

Chapter 7

O - Organizing and Balancing Your Life. Yes, it's possible.

"Life balance means balancing the outer success of achievement with the inner success of family and personal growth."
-Linda and Richard Eyre, authors of *Life Balance*

Look into the eyes of any graduate and you'll see pride and joy. They have learned so much, grown in myriad ways, and discovered what it's like to accomplish something really powerful. They've worked hard and can now enter the next challenge, a new phase of life.

To graduate from high school, college, or even kindergarten nowadays, you have to work very hard at juggling plenty of books, information, and relationships. A lot of planning leads to graduation day. It doesn't just happen all by itself.

What has to be done to graduate from college? First you have to get good grades in high school to get accepted into college. You have to balance a lot of books on your head and study. Remember when Mom put a couple of books on your head and you tried to take a few steps? Whoa. You had to stay centered and balanced. You need enough money to pay for tuition. In my case, I worked two or three jobs starting in high school and still had big student loans. You have to show up - consistently. You have to navigate your way through relationships. Is he the greatest love of my life or just another jerk disguised as a decent guy? You have to plan and organize your time wisely -- remembering to fit in some fun too. C'mon, let's not forget the parties. You do all this so you can graduate.

Throughout our lives, we graduate many times. Whenever we decide to explore new avenues we graduate from our old ways of doing things and move into the unknown realm of possibility. It's exciting and scary all at the same time.

Why Do We Need to be Balanced?

In a 2003, a special report conducted by the National Association of Female Executives found that 83 percent of the women surveyed said it is more difficult to juggle all their responsibilities than it was five years ago. Seventy-eight percent of the women thought borders between their personal lives and work lives were blurred. We keep getting more technically savvy and obtaining timesaving gadgets. Yet, we are still overwhelmed and find balancing difficult.

I'm concerned about women's health in America. We run at a frantic pace year in and year out and take on entirely too many obligations. Our health is getting poorer.

- 1 in 3 women and 1 in 2 men will have cancer in his/her lifetime.

- 1 in 8 American women will be diagnosed with breast cancer.

- Depression is very common among women. It affects nearly 20 percent of women worldwide.

- Diabetes will increase 165% over the next 50 years, with 29 million Americans diagnosed.
  Our children are unhealthy too.

- Over 8 million children have asthma, up 232% in the last 40 years.

- Obesity has doubled in the last 20 years. 1 in 4 children are obese.

- In the last 20 years, Type 2 diabetes among children has increased 10 fold.

- By age 12, 70% of children have developed beginning stages of hardening on the arteries.

These statistics are alarming. They show us we have a tremendous opportunity to care better for our loved ones and ourselves.

There are so many different people and cultures in the world. Talking to people from around the globe has taught me that everyone really wants the same things.

- Happiness or Contentment

- Success

- Love

- Peace -- a safe world to live in

The thing is, success means different things to different people. Living a balanced life is what brings you true joy. You need to figure out just what that balance is.

As I traveled around the world, I've discovered how other people balance and live their lives. The Spanish and Italians have siesta where they get together with family or friends during the day and socialize. The British have tea time. British people get three or four weeks of holiday (vacation) in their first year of work. In America we're lucky to get that after 10 years of service.

America continues to be the fastest paced society. We run and run and run and where are we going? For what do we labor so hard? These are fundamental questions to ponder in your search for balance.

- ❑ Why do you have/want to have children?
- ❑ Why do you do what you're doing, day in and day out?
- ❑ Why do you work?
- ❑ Are you content with your life? If not, what needs to change?
- ❑ What are you willing to sacrifice or give up to get what you want?

If you're like most people, the choices are endless. Work commitments, family schedules, hobbies, exercise, church, and volunteering all tug at our time like a receding tide. We run in and out after the tide. There is hope. You have the capacity to balance yourself, to set your own priorities and agenda. Our influence over ourselves can be far stronger than any other influence.

It takes a firm commitment to create balancing and re-prioritize. You have to accept that you have a part to play in the madness or the joyfulness. You are responsible for yourself and your family and you can achieve the type of life you truly desire.

If You Fail to Plan, You're Planning to Fail

*Decide what you want, decide what you are willing
to exchange for it. Establish your priorities and go to work.*
-H. L. Hunt

Let's get real about balance. Is balance achievable in our unbalanced world? Some say yes, some say no. Balance is achieved when we feel harmony with others and ourselves. To expect this every moment of every day is crazy and perhaps a little delusional.

Being in balance feels like a profound peace, a sense that you are doing the right thing at the right time. That feeling, however, is fleeting and is countered with times of imbalance, which awaken in us our deep-seated beliefs and values. Something isn't right. But what? We have to explore to figure out how we can make our life right for us. Leaders don't wait for others to figure this out for them. They figure it out for themselves. If you fail to plan, you're planning to fail. So the goal may not be a perfect balance like on a justice scale but a plan for life balancing.

How to SCORE© and Win!

(Or at least die trying - only kidding)

*"The trouble with not having a goal is that you can spend your
life running up and down the field and never scoring."*
- Bill Copeland

Let's look at how we can make beautiful things happen and shape our own future. The SCORE philosophy will educate you on the fine art of balancing.

S - Set priorities
C - Control Chaos
O - Organize your million things
R - Rejuvenate yourself
E - Equalize and Balance

S - Set Priorities

To choose well and set priorities, we have to be aware that we have tons of options every day. Consequently, we must admit to ourselves that we can not do everything today! We know we can't "do it all" and yet, every time we turn around we feel like someone else is doing it better than us.

In Chapter Three, you had the opportunity to clarify your priorities. Now would be a good time to review your answers and double-check yourself before proceeding.

As I mentioned in Chapter Three, I put myself first, and some people – particularly Moms -- are surprised by this. The way I figure, if it weren't for me and my husband, the kids wouldn't exist. I believe in the "oxygen-mask" principle. You know when you're on a plane and the flight attendant tells you to put on your mask first and then help your children or other people. I truly believe the only way I can support and lead others is if I am whole and healthy myself. It took me a long time to realize this. I used to give and give and give and then resent others, get sick, and say, "Why doesn't anyone ever take care of me?" (Have you ever said that?)

However, let me make this perfectly clear. My needs do not come first to the exclusion of others' needs. As a Momager, everyone's needs are taken into account and I make sacrifices of my time, career, hobbies, and interests for what is best for my family. We have to make room in our family for everyone's needs to be met some of the time. Not all of the time. Some of my career goals have become long-term instead of trying to pursue my career full-time while my children were young. My family is a top priority and I have always fit my career in around my family's needs. You can see why flexibility is so very important to balancing.

When you're a leader and your role is to serve, you need to take care of yourself and have plenty of energy to be able to give to others.

While reviewing the priorities that you ranked in Chapter Three, you may have found some inconsistencies. Usually people rank family as the #1 priority, but many of them discover that family ranks third or fourth in terms of how much time or thought they actually give to it.

If we're inconsistent between our values and our actions, we are almost guaranteed to feel off balance. Get to know what you really value and then align it with your actions and you'll be so much more balanced. If you truly value career and your own interests as your top two priorities, then I would encourage you to think long and hard about bringing children into the world. If you are going to have children, family needs to be a top priority.

Priorities Change

If it's not one thing it's another.

Imagine that you have a fruit bowl that is large enough to hold six pieces of fruit. Now, think about what your priorities were *before* you had kids. Your list might include:

- Self - Banana (Think long and lean)

- Career - Pineapple

- Friends - Pear

- Original family – (Mom, Dad, brothers, and/or sisters) - Grapes and yes, there are black grapes in the family

- Home/Apartment -Orange

- Loving relationship with boyfriend or husband – Apple

Then you had a child or two or three, and your priorities began to change. You had to make room for the kids in the fruit bowl. But the bowl was already full. What did you give up or sacrifice? Did you cut out your relationship with your husband? Did you decide to cut the career in half and work less hours? Or did you just try to cram the kids in there without seriously planning how you were going to make it work? Most women try to cram it all in and make it work. Sooner or later the fruit spoils and you realize you can't do it that way any more.

To balance based on your top priorities you must know your priorities and make the appropriate sacrifices. It involves being intentional with the choices you make and planning based on those priorities. When there are major shifts in priorities, everything needs to be altered. When your kids go away to school, or when your parents get older and ultimately die, or when someone loses his or her job, you must change and rebalance. Do what's most important to you and live your life "on purpose."

It's Always Something. . .

You will have your own line-up of priorities. If your top priorities are work and interests above self and family, you are going to have trouble with relationships. People come first and then career. Your priorities come first and then based on your priorities, you can schedule your activities.

When your priorities are clear, you can make choices about your time and say "no" to anything that doesn't fit into your top priorities. You will know you are doing the most important things and that taking on additional tasks won't really give you joy. This gives you the freedom to choose between all the requests made of you.

C - Control Chaos

"Imbalance keeps us moving. If you can learn to laugh whenever you trip, teeter, or fall, you'll start to appreciate how much a misstep can teach you."
Author unknown

We are bombarded with information, media, and choices all the time. A *USA Today* article, "Choice Overload Burdens Daily Modern

Life." highlights how difficult it is to decide what we want. With all these choices our satisfaction with the decisions we make is decreasing.

As available options increase:

- People are more likely to regret their decisions.
- People are more likely to anticipate regretting their decisions. The anticipation prevents people from actually deciding.
- Expectations about how good the decision will be go up, and reality doesn't meet.
- When decisions have disappointing results, people tend to blame themselves.

Top Ten Ways to Control the Chaos

1. Change your thinking so you don't have chaotic thoughts. Think of one thing at a time. Stay focused and positive. If a task or situation is difficult, recognize that and don't give up. Persevere. Say, "I can. It's challenging, but possible."
2. Simplify your life. Be content with who you are and what you already have. We have to learn how to be satisfied with "good enough" instead of always seeking the best. Strive for contentment, not busyness. Realize that every possession and responsibility requires time and care.
3. Break down your goals into baby steps. Do just one or two steps at a time. We're so good at multi-tasking that we sometime get carried away and do three or four things at a time, which often leads to greater stress as important details fall through the cracks.
4. Live in day-tight compartments. Plan for the future but LIVE in the present.
5. Experience the power of your feelings. Acknowledge them, let them rise to the surface, express them, and then let them go. Trapped feelings make us feel overwhelmed. Tiredness is emotionally induced 90 percent of the time. Express yourself!
6. Pray daily - that you can handle the chaos you are experiencing and/or be relieved of it if the burden is too heavy. Pray before

you commit to any additional tasks. Pray that you can do what the Creator wants you to do, and eliminate all other unnecessary work.

7. Instead of asking "Why me?" ask "What can I learn from this?" Recognize all experiences contain lessons.

8. When you *do* make a mistake, don't beat yourself up over it. Kim Langley, President of Life Balance says, *"Make it a habit to catch people in the act of doing things right - beginning with yourself."* An eagle misses 70 percent of its strikes and is a powerful creature. Don't scold yourself mentally. If you know you have perfectionistic tendencies, make a mistake on purpose so you can see that you'll survive and things will still work out.

9. Do what you think and feel is best, no matter what people think of you. Be thankful for what is good in your choices, rather than regretful about what is disappointing. Do your best and leave the rest.

10. Use a simple time-management system. Avoid complicated gizmos unless you understand how to use them and are sure they will save you time. If using a PDA (Personal Digital Assistant or organizer), enter calendar information daily, but also print out weekly and monthly versions to see the "big picture." Identify overly committed days or upcoming weeks. Try to rearrange them or get ready for hectic times.

11. Act boldly and as if it were impossible to fail. (I just couldn't stop at ten!)

O - Organize Your Million Things

Most of us have too much "stuff." All your possessions require time and energy to store and maintain. Remember: Less is Best.

Top Ten Ideas for Organizing Your "Stuff"

❑ Find a place for everything. Have a well-defined, well-confined place for every possession. Put things back where they belong. Find a home for everything you own or give it to charity.

❑ Only touch a piece of paper once. Immediately find where it belongs or throw it away. I open my mail over the wastebasket and get rid of a lot of mail without even opening it. If you collect stray paperwork, keep it in one pile, not in multiple places. Schedule a "de-clutter" time every day or once a week.

❑ Take a good hard look at your home or office. Wherever you see clutter, piles, or gathering spaces, attack them within a confined time frame. I can look at a pile for only one week and then it has to be addressed.

❑ Establish a file for each person and pet in the household. Each family member's legal documents, report cards, medical records, and other important papers go into his or her file..

❑ Store "like items" together. All computer stuff in a basket. All CD's on a rack, all cleaning supplies in one closet. You get the idea.

❑ De-clutter every year. Pretend you're going to move and decide what you really must keep and what would cost too much to move. If you haven't worn it or used it in a year, get rid of it.

❑ Don't procrastinate. It can take more time and energy to wait, then to do the task. If you don't know what to do next, ask someone for direction. Honey, do you still want this 1970's pair of green pants? (Don't ask unless you really want to know.)

❑ Work within time compartments. Give yourself a certain amount of time to complete each task. I usually spend no more than 10-15 minutes at a time tidying up. For repetitive tasks, try to beat your best score. This is really fun around the house. Can you believe we do the dishes in 5 minutes and 27 seconds?

❑ Do a trade. When one new item comes into the house/ office, get rid of one old item.

❑ Be thankful for what you have. If you are truly grateful for all that you have, you will find contentment where you are.

R - Reward Yourself!

You can increase your power and energy by pausing to reflect on the wonderful job you're already doing. Feel the power of comfort. Once in a while, reward yourself with time, thoughts, and actions that are rejuvenating.

Top 10 Ways to Reward Yourself

❑ Take a deep breath. As a matter of fact, splurge, take a *few* deep breaths. Close your eyes and take 10 breaths, slowly inhaling through your nose and exhaling through your mouth.

❑ Feel and appreciate your one and only body. Exercise. Invest time in your health. Take a short walk - and breathe deeply. Stretch often.

❑ Laugh. Keep a book of jokes within reach, and post some favorite cartoons nearby. Remember you're not only one in a million. You're one in six billion!

❑ Love. Get together with family or friends. Call or go out to lunch, talk, share your challenges and triumphs. Have a "date night" with your significant other. Keep up with your girlfriends.

❑ Enjoy a cup of tea or other favorite beverage. Sip it slowly. Smell the aroma.

❑ Plan and take a mini-vacation. Mentally or physically. Visualize yourself in a pleasant scene -- lounging in a mountain meadow, relaxing at the beach, or swinging in a hammock.

❑ Pause to enjoy your food. Indulge in a little something you really love - like rich dark chocolate, or fresh fruit or nuts. Notice the words are "a little something." Despite what advertisers would like you to believe, you *can* get too much of a good thing!

❑ Get a massage or give yourself one. Use your favorite lotion to rub your feet, temples, shoulders, and the back of your neck. Do neck rolls.

❑ Listen to inspiring music. Fit it to your mood.

❑ Remember your victories. Talk about them, relive them. Give yourself a hug or pat on the back once in a while. A friend of mine wakes up, looks at herself in the mirror and says, "Good morning gorgeous!" Can you imagine what your outlook would be like if you did that every day?

E - Equalize and Balance Life

> *"It is woman who keeps the world in balance."*
> Mrs. Chalkstone, suffragist

In Chapter Three, you did an exercise called The Wheel of Life. Take a moment to review the assessment that you completed so you are clear about how your time is currently being divided.

Five Steps to Chart a Road Map for Balancing

One pre-requisite to begin balancing is to determine who is in control of your life. Are you responsible for your thoughts, words, and actions or is someone else? Some people blame their outlook and behaviors on things they believe are out of their control. They blame their parents, boss, or environment for how they are today. They say things like, "My father was an alcoholic and that's why I can't deal with . . ." This is simply not true.

If you want things to change, look in the mirror, not out the window. Try one of those super-magnifying bathroom mirrors? Whoa. You'll find a few blemishes. Look at yourself and what you are doing. Change yourself and then other things begin to shift.

You are responsible for yourself, your attitude, and your behavior. You must believe that you and God are in full control. The Creator gave you your intellect, reasoning abilities, body, spirit and everything you are. You have been designed for a very special reason. Claim the power you have been given to fulfill your purpose and leave a legacy.

Step 1: Long Range Goals

- Once a year plan some uninterrupted time to set your yearly goals.
- Think long-term. What do you want to achieve during the next year?
- Are you content? If not, what needs to change?

These questions should be answered in the context of what is going to really matter in ten, fifteen, or even fifty years from now.

You might want to plan five to ten years ahead. Personally, I have trouble planning that far in advance, but it sets the framework for doing what's really important. We have to focus on the top priorities and let the rest go away for the time being.

What will you do?

Journal and write down what you want to focus on for the next year. If you don't have a journal, get one or grab some paper. You can have as many goals as you want. However, try to keep them simple and achievable with a stretch and some hard work. I usually focus on five SMART goals. Remember? SMART goals are Specific, Measurable, Achievable, Realistic, and Timebound.

- What goals are you going to set?

- How will you attain them?

- When will you set these goals?

Instead of making New Year's Resolutions on December 31, I set my resolutions in September. New Year's Eve is a lot less stressful now. I already have goals that I've been working on for a few months! Ha - I'm ahead of the game. After the kids are back in school each Autumn, I begin thinking about my life and what I want to accomplish in the upcoming year.

Your birthday is also a good time to focus on yearly planning. Why not give yourself the best gift and celebrate how far you've come in the past year and look ahead to planning the future? This is a time of dreaming and then turning the dreams into reality.

Who will help you?

Delegate and ask for help. As Momagers, we need to ask for help and accept it when offered. Assign who is going to do what. This is a critical step because no one makes it in this world alone. We all need each other and have to rely on each other for help or guidance. Often, thinking about who your strategic partners are going to be opens up your horizons and eliminates the "I have to do it all myself" blues. Think about when you are going to begin and complete each goal and what success will look like.

This type of thinking can be fun and creative, but it is also hard mental work. If you have difficulty coming up with written goals, then start by drawing pictures. I usually mind map and start with a core issue and work around it. Sometimes drawing pictures about feelings you have toward a certain goal can unblock creativity.

Start with the end result and then work your way backward until you know all the steps you need to take and in what order. Write all the steps down until you have items you can work on today.

Mind Mapping

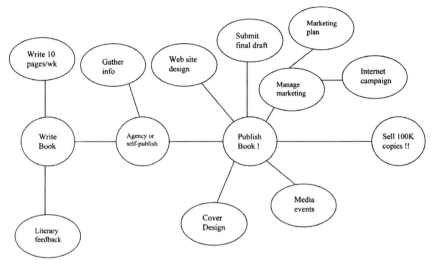

Examples:

Goal # 1:   Sell 100,000 copies of this book by Dec. 31, 2005.
   (Thanks for helping me reach my goal!)

- Finish manuscript by Feb. 2004 (Oops. Plan changed --it was finished in April '04).
- Determine self-publishing or going with agency by March 2004.
- Do radio/TV shows to promote the book.
- Organize book signings with top 10 bookstores.

Goal # 2:   Strengthen relationship with extended family/friends
Ideas:

- List members – Aunt Erika and Uncle John
- Decide which holidays we will spend together.
- Call once a week.
- Buy and install a computer monitor with pictures by February so we can see each other once a week.
- Plan coffee dates via computer or phone calls.
- Commit to problem solving and apologize the same day an offense occurs.

Yearly planning lets you focus on your top priorities. You can then relax and realize you have plenty of time to accomplish your goals. It relieves you of feeling like you have to do everything today. Assigning people to help you also expands your support network and strategic partners.

Step 2 – Monthly Goals

Think about what you want to accomplish during the next month. Your monthly goals will be determined from your list of goals for the year. Bob and I also look at the month ahead together. We call ourselves the "family leadership team." We keep a family calendar and look at it on the first Sunday of the month and think about what is on the schedule and fill in anything we forgot.

One of my yearly goals is to show my husband more appreciation.

For that goal, my monthly goals might be:

January: Give Bob three compliments a week. "Thank you, honey..."

February: Greet Bob with a smile and hug in the morning. (It was amazing to see his shocked look at first. Now, it's a warm way to start the day).

March: Tell Bob how much I trust his judgement. (Always a real winner!)

Rearrange your monthly schedule if things look too tight. Certain months are busier than others are. Usually May, August, September, and December are hectic times for us with the school schedule and holidays, so to avoid being bombarded, we spread out the other major tasks earlier or later in the year.

Step 3 - Weekly Goals

On Sunday, I plan the week ahead and think about the week as a complete time frame. I plan all my major priorities like prayer time, exercise, work, and quality time with my husband. The kids' events are discussed and we decide who's going to drop them off and pick them up.

I think of this Sunday planning time like filling the gas tank in the car. I try to fill up on "high-test," so we can run smoothly through the week. This strategy ensures I'm planning life according to my priorities, not anyone else's. For instance, sometimes the goals are as lofty as "exercise three times this week" or as simple as "whisper and cuddle with each child this week."

Step 4 - Daily Goals

Balance is a daily fine-tuning job. Spending just five minutes a day prioritizing and goal setting will make a major difference in your life. If you've got more time to spend, great.

Gloria Estephan, mother of two and singer says; "Every morning, my husband, Emilio and I drive over to the Cardozo Hotel. We'll walk for three miles on the beach there. And I always enjoy sitting at the bar of the hotel where we've had some incredible celebrations over the years." (*Good Housekeeping*, Jan. '04)

Answer these three questions every day:

1. What is one goal I can accomplish today in the top priority areas? Self, family, and work.

2. What can I do to be balanced and have more fun?

3. What does God want me to do today? Try to stay open and flexible because your plan may be changed by God's will.

Journal and Pray Your Way to Greater Happiness

Daily, I journal and pray (Okay, I admit - *most* mornings) for at least 30 minutes. I get up early so I can have quiet time to organize my thinking, plan my day, and set my daily goals. If something's bothering me, I'll wake up even earlier so I have time to contemplate what's going on, and begin working through it. The way I figure, getting up early is better than missing sleep at night because my mind knows I'll work it out in the morning.

It took about five years for me to finally see the benefits of journaling. The emotional security and ability to pour forth ideas and feelings has totally changed how I deal with people and situations.

A study conducted by the University of California and the University of Miami found that people who keep a daily journal of what they're thankful for, sleep better, are more optimistic, and feel a stronger sense of connection to loved ones than those who dwell on daily hassles. Spend a couple minutes each day reflecting on at least five things that you're thankful for (they can be situations, people, conversations, ideas, events . . . anything at all) and write them down. You will find you're enjoying life more than ever and you're reaching for new goals.

Journaling helps you to be emotionally stronger. It gives you greater clarity about your feelings and beliefs. As women, we have such deep feelings and emotions. If we don't express them in a healthy way, they come out in other areas of our life. We become irritable, snap at people, and sometimes "blow," as my husband lovingly calls it.

Our emotions are like a teakettle. When the water gets hot, you have to open a release valve to let the steam out slowly. When you get boiling hot, your whistle's going to blow. So, control the heat by releasing your emotions before you boil. If you let some steam off daily. you can control the screeching of the whistle.

Keep a planner and each day block out thirty to sixty minutes of "down time." Doing this will give you time to just be you. This is *your* time. Do something spontaneous, pray, call a friend, take a walk in the woods, meditate, shop, or just do *nothing*. Take mini-vacations often to relieve the tensions and stress of life.

If you're thinking, "There's no way I can fit in thirty minutes or an hour a day," you're still not committed enough to balancing your life. You're just too busy and need to reprioritize so you have more time to recharge. Using every spare second is *not* the object of the game. *The object of the game of life is to have joy, faith, make a contribution, and love.*

Now someone is bound to ask, "Do you mean to tell me I have to do this every single day? I can't even find the time to exercise, or talk to my partner and you want me to fit in one more thing." And the answer is No. You don't HAVE to do anything. What will happen is you will find you WANT to take the time because everything else in your life will become clearer and run so much more smoothly.

Step 5 –Affirm and Imagine Your Goals in Present Tense

Affirm for yourself everything that you want. Imagine your wishes and desires as vividly as possible. Claim your goals and dreams. You can take any of your goals and positively tell yourself you are living it.

Guided imagery can also help you in any type of healing process. Images affect the body in profound ways. This is because, as guided imagery pioneer <u>Belleruth Naparstek</u> says, "images in the mind are real events to the body." These images can change you physically and mentally.

Benefits of Guided Imagery

Numerous guided imagery studies with cancer patients showed that patients had less pain, felt more positive, and lived longer with regular guided imagery practice.

You can also learn to focus better and reduce stress with guided imagery. The act of sitting quietly and breathing deeply is a form of meditation. And the more you imagine yourself in a safe place, or hear a tinkling fountain, or picture yourself relaxing every part of your body, the more your body learns how to focus and let go. And when you focus and let go you can experience change more rapidly and feel more in control of your life.

Imagery can help you change your food behaviors and help people with eating disorders or compulsive overeating to heal. With guided imagery, you can change the images you have in your mind that make you overeat. It's a great tool to help you change your life. If you haven't done guided imagery before, I recommend you consider it.

For example:

- I am enjoying good health and exercise.
- I am learning from each new experience, positive or negative.
- I appreciate abundance and have everything I want.
- I am having more fun every day.
- I can handle everything that comes my way today.
- I am at peace with myself and everyone I meet.

Be Flexible

"Living is a form of not being sure, not knowing what next or how
. . .
We guess. We may be wrong, but we take leap after leap in the
dark."
Agnes DeMille, dancer & choreographer

Like mighty oak trees and graceful dancers, we must be flexible. If our goals or plans change along the way, that's okay. One closed door always leads to another open window. Life is always changing. If we are too stiff we will break. With high winds and lots of pressure, the oak tree bends and accommodates to the forces of nature. So, too, must you be flexible. It's so true that life is what happens while you're making other plans. Be aware of what is happening and stay open to what you receive. You may find you get more than you even asked for.

Be Thankful!

There's something magical about gratitude. The more grateful we are, the more we receive. In 1998, a girlfriend gave me a gratitude journal and told me to write down five things I was grateful for every day and to never repeat the same things. (Was it on Oprah that year?) At first, I put down the usual things like family, friends, health, and living in America. Well, those ran out after the third day and then I was stuck.

Changing perspectives really altered me. I had to look for things to be grateful for. To stop taking people and things for granted. And guess what? I found more and more blessings every time I turned around. I received and continue to receive more thankful moments than I ever experienced before. You will too.

Martin Seligman, author of *Authentic Happiness* found that people who are grateful and express their thankfulness have higher levels of happiness. He teaches a course in Positive Psychology and conducts a "Gratitude Night." Class members bring a guest who has been important in their lives, and who they've never fully thanked. They present a testimonial about that person followed by discussion. The night fills everyone with power and awe. Participants discover how vital it is to their happiness to appreciate and thank the people in their lives.

Many students comment that "Gratitude night was one of the greatest nights of my life." Most participants felt happier for the next several days. "The reason gratitude works to increase life satisfaction is that it amplifies good memories about the past: their intensity, frequency, and the tag lines the memories have."

The first controlled experiment was to randomly assign people to keep a daily diary for two weeks, either of grateful happenings, difficulties, or just life events. Joy happiness, and life satisfaction shot up for the gratitude group.

When we are truly, deeply grateful for all our gifts, our life becomes more rich and full. Being grateful for the small things we and other people do brings us abundance. It gives our life deeper meaning. So look for all the small things that bring you joy.
Here's a peak at a few of the entries in my gratitude journal.

- Tina's excited sparkling eyes
- The smell and first sip of pumpkin coffee
- The stillness and quiet of morning
- Sharing freshly baked scones
- God, for giving me more perseverance
- The gentle encouraging voice of my friend
- Feeling proud of David as he willingly found books to give to charity
- Holding Bob's strong hands during church

Live in the moment, search for blessings, and you will find plenty to be grateful for. Always, always, always, be thankful.

Be Multi-faceted

Don't become boring and one-dimensional. You know you have six areas of life to continually balance. No wonder it's so hard sometimes. The balancing comes in juggling all these areas. When we focus on only one of the areas we become "one-dimensional." Look at any drawing or painting that is one-dimension and it is flat, boring, and uninteresting. Gaze into a diamond or gemstone. The facets are what make it brilliantly sparkle.

You've met plenty of one-dimensional people. They focus on work to the exclusion of their family. They focus on their children to the exclusion of themselves. They volunteer so much they have no time for their spouse. The combinations of imbalance are endless.

These wise words by Mahatma Gandhi remind us to focus on being whole, well-balanced people. "One man cannot do right in one department of life whilst he is occupied doing wrong in any other department. Life is one indivisible whole."

The benefits of being balanced are more satisfaction and joy with our homes, our work places, and ourselves. I hope you'll be honest about what matters most to you, and use your time accordingly. Our most precious resource is time and it's always slipping away from us. Time is so fleeting. Organizing and balancing helps us use our precious time wisely. When we are balanced, life can be a lot more peaceful and we can live it as a celebration of joy. Every single day can be a time to explore new opportunities. Celebrate what you've already accomplished and look forward to growing in the future.

Chapter 8

R - Resolve Problems and Deal with Conflict

*"Motherhood brings as much joy as ever,
but is still brings boredom, exhaustion and sorrow too.
Nothing else ever will make you as happy or as sad, as proud or as tired,
for nothing is quite as hard as helping a person develop his own individuality -
especially while you struggle to keep your own."*
-Marguerite Kelly & Elia Parsons

Life is full of fires. Momagers have to be great problem solvers so they can put out the fires whenever and wherever they flare up. In addition to being "fire-fighters," we're referees, judges, and medics. Mothering requires fine-tuned conflict management skills because problem solving is part of daily life. If we teach peaceful problem solving to our children, they will bring those skills into the world. Don't you think we need more compassionate leaders to promote world peace? It all starts in the home and moves outward.

Ask any Mom who has dealt with a two-year-old or teenager and she'll tell you that temper tantrums, and "melt-downs" are part and parcel of their life. Just the word discipline conjures up pictures and emotions that are fiery hot. An effective Momager knows that fires have to be put out quickly and properly or people can get burned.

From the time each of my kids were 18 months to 36 months old, I had to deal with an enormous range of emotions. Their emotions and mine - simultaneously. Nothing prepared me for the anger, elation, embarrassment, and downright passion I would feel for these children. Sometimes the fire got "out of control."

Let me set the stage. One day I was shopping with my two toddlers. David was four years old and Tina was 23 months old. I hadn't been shopping for anything other than groceries for over four years. This day, I felt brave. My strategy was to take them to a small Christian bookstore and just browse for 15 minutes. "How much trouble can they get in?"

Before we entered the store we reviewed the three rules again. Rule Number One: Stay with Mommy. Rule Number Two: Use a quiet voice. And Rule Number Three, Don't "get the gimmies." Don't say, "Can you "gimme" this or "gimme' that?"

So, we're walking around the bookstore and I put on headphones to listen to some music. Gee, what kind of music are people listening to these days? Perhaps this will be my first re-entry back into popular culture. I select a song, look down, and both kids are gone! It couldn't have been more than 19 seconds. Frantically, I start calling them in a hushed voice, "David, Tina, come to Mommy." I don't see or hear anything. So I walk briskly up and down the aisles with no success.

Aha! A clerk is in the inspirational journal section. "Have you seen two little children? "They were just with me." I embarrassingly admit. Already I know there's no "Mother Of The Year" award for me. We search everywhere with no success. By this time I am fuming! "When I find those kids I'm going to . . ." Ooops, I'm supposed to be a mother that is the picture of grace and peace, especially here.

I hear some rustling. I look in a narrow path which is the storefront window and there are my two little "angels" destroying the book store display. Books are strewn on the floor, posters are half off the wall. The display is ruined. "How could they do this in just a few minutes?"

I can't fit in the tiny opening to get them so I forcefully, yet lovingly, say: "David Andrew, come here right now!" He looks up at me and goes back to "playing." Now, I blow, "David and Tina get over here right now or I will kill you!" The teenagers working in the store look at me as if I've lost my mind. I burst into tears.

To make a long story short - that day I learned how out of control I could get if I didn't deal with conflict and my authority properly. Every mother that has been through the terrible two's or the teenage years can relate. You know what it's like to deal with heat that seems unbearable. "How could two small children humiliate me and turn me into a raving lunatic?" I had so much to learn. But not to worry. My kids were determined to teach me.

The secret is out. Life is full of problems. In every group of people, conflict exists. Whether it's with a work team, marriage partner, or children, people have different opinions. Those differences can make us feel hot, sticky, unbearably uncomfortable, and cause a "fire in our belly." Face it. You are going to have to "put out a few fires." Maybe "Fire Woman" should be a new superhero, what do you think?

Fortunately, we can learn how to solve problems so we can manage the fires and put out most of them when they are still small.

What are the Sources of Conflict?

Conflicts arise out of differences between people, goals, values, and ways of doing things. Sometimes we just wake up on the wrong side of the bed, know we're cranky, and have more internal conflict.

Conflict in your family team can exist for any of the following reasons:

- Schedules
- Priorities
- Personalities
- Family structure
- Competition for attention and funds
- Ineffective communication
- Status and authority
- _____(Add your own reasons here)
- _____ (C'mon add more . . .)

Conflict can occur for hundreds of different reasons. Anything from, "Mom, he looked at me!" to "She took my gum" can rapidly erupt into a full-scale drama if I don't deal with it immediately. Because life happens so fast and often unexpectedly, we have to invest time and energy exploring different problem solving techniques so we're ready for anything. Doing this helps all our family members feel valued and appreciated.

Conflict can be viewed in two ways. Positive or Negative. Actually, the conflict, itself, is neutral. How you deal with conflict determines whether the outcome is positive or negative for you and your family.

"Conflict is negative." People from this camp believe conflict is a major cause of stress and fear. Conflict is caused by troublemakers. Conflict is bad. Conflict should be avoided at all costs. Reacting to conflict can be incredibly draining, stressful, and time consuming. People choose sides, territories develop, and no one wins. Conflict destroys morale and cooperation.

"Conflict is positive." Some leaders see conflict as useful. Conflict is a natural result of change and working with other people. They think conflict uncovers "status quo" beliefs and brings about needed change and improvements. The by-product of conflict is problem solving and, if done properly, explores new ways of doing things. Quite often, changes for the best can only be uncovered after there is a conflict. Conflict can and should be managed.

You have a choice as to how you view conflict. Effective leaders see that conflict can have some difficult moments, but is positive if it is handled properly. Leaders who see conflict positively usually see opportunities and issues instead of problems.

I've seen amazing transformation happen after conflict exists. Unfortunately, I've also seen the crippling effects that occur when people feel discouraged or demoralized. You have much power when dealing with conflicts and solving problems. Make sure you use your power wisely. What you do today will affect generations to come.

I usually begin my conflict seminars with an exercise that creates conflict. Two co-workers are given some money, either a $20, $50 or $100 bill. They have three minutes to decide who gets to keep the money. Well, you should see the negotiating and bartering and even pleading that follows. People make up heart-wrenching stories about their sick aunt or starving child or whatever else they can think of to get the money. It's amazing to see how creative people are when they have conflict and want to resolve it. Sometimes people yell, call each other names, and even threaten each other. The clever people usually cooperate and come up with a win-win solution. They offer to split the money and both people win.

How you deal with conflict can be rewarding if done properly and devastating, if done wrong. That's why it is so critical that Momagers learn how to accept and resolve conflict. Learning how to resolve conflict in a healthy way helps you get the most out of your family and yourself.

Being able to deal with conflict and resolve problems are necessary skills for any leader.

How to Solve Problems Swiftly and with Long-term Change

This four-step process contains the magic of solving problems while retaining everyone's self-esteem. It can be used at home or at work. Teach your kids how to use it to solve their own problems.

Step One

What is the Problem?

"Every problem has in it the seeds of its own solution."
Norman Vincent Peale

The first step in successfully solving a problem or conflict is defining it. Everyone has to be clear about what the problem is. It's critical to change your mindset to seeing challenges and problems as opportunities, not obstacles. Of course, no blaming is allowed. Blaming only puts people on the defensive and doesn't positively affect the outcome.

There are four parts to consider:

- Let each person *share* his or her view and listen to others' viewpoints. Understanding becomes much deeper if you have each person state the problem from another person's perspective. "If you were John, what does the problem look like from his angle?" This strategy also breaks down barriers and everyone

157

knows they will be heard and maybe even understood. Would that be novel?

- Problem *defined*. After everyone has shared his or her perspective write down a problem statement. Keep it short, simple, and clear. No more than 15 words. Be sure everyone is in agreement as to what the problem really is.
- State the problem *objectively* and factually. Try not to slant the situation toward any bias. It should be a simple statement of fact. Keep it limited and small enough so you can solve it. Don't "throw in the kitchen sink" by including more than one issue at a time.
- Identify the *solution* desired in measurable terms.

Problem Defined
The kitchen is messy after dinner.
Solution Desired:
The kitchen will be clean (not spotless) by 7:30 p.m.
(In a *cheerful* manner, would be icing on the cake.)

Step Two

What is Causing the Problem?

Much like an investigation team finds out what caused a fire, you must determine what caused the issue you want to solve. Dig deep for the true root cause(s).
Answer these three questions:

- What are the potential cause(s)?
- What are the most likely cause(s)?
- What is/are the true root cause(s)?

Step Three

What are Possible Solutions?

This is the moment we've all been waiting for. It's time to solve the problem. Instead of looking at constraints and rules, open your mind to creative options. Think of all the ways you can to solve the problem.

Brainstorming works great here. Brainstorming is a freethinking technique. Here are basic ground rules to make it effective.

1. Don't discount anyone's ideas. Avoid criticism.
2. Your goal is to gather as many ideas as possible. Go for quantity. List at least ten possible solutions. The more, the merrier.
3. Look for wild/exaggerated ideas. Sometimes, the most farfetched ideas actually work, or lead to other solutions that work.
4. Try to build on the ideas of others (when in groups).
5. Make a list.

The brainstorming step in problem solving requires the most creativity, so have fun with it. Include everyone that is affected by the problem in this process. Giving input at these early stages will ensure they "buy in" and will be part of the solution.

Review all solutions and then begin eliminating choices. Rule out all ideas that will not produce the desired result. Look at the benefits and effort needed to implement the top ideas. Decide what obstacles might exist. What resources, both financial and "human," can you assign to the plan? Determine outcomes of each top idea. Who will this option affect? Then ask the question, "With all the information we have right now, what is the best choice?" It's so important that this step includes a personal commitment to the plan.

Step Four

Select the Best Solution and Make a Plan to Implement it

Hooray! You've made it to this point. Now you can decide on the best solution and have everyone commit to it. Commit to it -- meaning marrying into the solution. Make a strategic plan to implement the solution. Start with the ideal target and work backward.

Who – Who are the people responsible for implementing the action steps?

What – What is expected as a change? Focus on observable behaviors.

Where – Where will meetings and follow-through take place?

When - Determine the time frame. Assign a start date and completion date for each step.

How – List the sequence of action steps.

Action Steps How?	Who?	Where?	What?	When started or completed?
Clear & wipe table	Steven	Kitchen or Dining Room	Surfaces clear and sanitized	6:30 p.m. start 7:30 complete
Clear counters & containers	David		Surfaces clear and sanitized	
Wash dishes	Tina Rose		Rinse & put in dishwasher	
Give praise & kisses (And finish the job after they're done)	Mom & Dad	Kitchen or loft	Show love~ They did it!	7:30 p.m.

Enjoy the environment in your family as you watch people solving problems and working together! You will feel great power and such a sense of joy in transforming your outlook and those of your family members. You will see more cooperation, responsible behavior, and greater trust. A common bond will connect you when you work through difficult situations with respect and dignity. "We have overcome" converts to "We can overcome."

"There is no doubt in my mind that there are many ways to be a winner,
but there is really only one way to be a loser, and that is to fail
and not look beyond the failure."
Kyle Rote Jr.

Family meetings are often the best times to solve family problems. Instead of complaining or nagging, now you can have family meetings where you can get everyone's input and make decisions.

Kids need to fail. They need to learn how to solve their own problems. They need to be able to control themselves and be in control of their own problems. When we make things easier for them and solve their problems, they don't get to experience a true sense of accomplishment. I know this can be uncomfortable for parents because we want to soften the blows and give them everything we didn't get. By softening the blows, we are making them weak problem solvers.

So, as Momagers, our leadership role is to assist others in their own problem solving. Ask them questions and teach them how to work through the problem solving steps.

Not only will you solve problems effectively, you will also teach your kids valuable conflict resolution techniques that can transfer to every aspect of life, from cleaning their rooms, to settling marital disputes, to getting employees to work together better.

One thing is for sure. The real world contains problems. Teach your children to solve problems and they will confidently enter the world. This problem solving approach ensures all people will be respected, included, and you can kiss your problems goodbye . . . Until of course, the next round begins. As Evander Holyfield says "A setback only paves the way for a comeback."

Abuse is Never Acceptable

"Being a mom can be so tough."
Julie Ann Barnhill, author of She's Gonna Blow.

In her book, Barnhill says there are three ways moms abuse their children and, with her permission, I have included her definitions and some of her insights in this section. The definition of abuse is *excessive or inappropriate behavior.* All of us have acted this way with our children at one time or another.

- **Physical abuse** – We always think abuse is beating or sexually assaulting children. Everything we do physically that is harmful or excessive is included in this category. You may not beat your child, but how about the way you roll your eyes, or look mad and ugly at them. How about if you grab their arm and hold on tightly even after you know they got the point? If you are angry and want your child to feel some of your pain, this is inappropriate. Or how about pushing your child or teasing them and shoving them occasionally. All these behaviors are a form of physical abuse.

Remember when your mom used to say, "Keep your face like that and it's going to freeze ugly." Well, the same applies to us moms as well. Yikes - I better buy a mirror.

- **Verbal abuse** – The things we're saying and how we say it. Have you ever compared your children to other kids? Comparing children sets up competition, sibling rivalry and a feeling of "I'm not good enough." Is that inappropriate behavior?

I grew up with four siblings. With four girls and only 11 months between my older sister and me, we were compared a lot. I hated it! I still do. Fortunately, now that we're adults our unique gifts and personalities have surfaced and we can appreciate those differences. (Most of the time that is.)

If each of us is unique and precious in God's eyes, why would we ever compare people? Each child has different gifts and talents. They have different personalities and timing for developing. It's only natural to want to know if your child is developing normally, but why all the pressure to keep up with what other children are doing? Try to hold your tongue and not compare. In our family we say, "It's not fair to compare." Our job as moms is not to fix our children and make them into something they are not. Our job is to love them and let God transform them into who they are meant to be.

Another form of verbal abuse is putting down kids. When Julie Barnhill's kids were young she used to sarcastically say, "Good job, Einstein." "Well I think most four year olds could do that." "Why can't you?" All these statements undermine a child's dignity and self-worth.

Let's address the topic of yelling. Mothers all feel exasperated at one time or another and yell. Once in a while it might be appropriate - if a child is crossing the street and a car is coming, or in other dangerous situations. What concerns me is when Moms yell a lot and berate their kids with yelling. Yelling can be harmful to kids. Repeated yelling harms moms too because they get emotionally distraught after a while. Yelling loses its impact if done often.

I am the product of parents who yelled a lot (Italians like to yell, they call it talking passionately). It has been extremely difficult to overcome the desire to scream at the kids when they don't listen or I'm angry.

When the children were younger, I found myself yelling as a discipline tool until I saw my youngest child, Steven cower in a corner and put his hands over his ears and cry. I looked at his dejected little body and it was just as bad as if I had physically hit him. His spirit and body were just crushed. The tongue can be stronger than a mighty sword and as Momagers we should be mirroring God's love for us. I don't think that includes yelling, screaming, ranting, and raving. Do you?

Try whispering instead of yelling. Now before you think I've gone off the deep end, stick with me. Think about this. What happens when someone whispers? We draw closer to them to hear What did they say? It peaks our curiosity. Are we going to hear something secret or classified? A whisper provokes a type of mystery and if we say, "I've got a secret for you" the child is even more interested in hearing what we have to say. Sometimes I clap my hands to get one of my kids' attention and then I whisper. It's amazing to see how whispering promotes a more respectful and peaceful home. Try it, you'll like it.

- **Spiritual abuse** – The things we do that spiritually hurt our children.
  We are a reflection of God to our children. We have a tremendous amount of responsibility. Sometimes the responsibility is overwhelming and we just want to leave. You can get stuck with who we are and where our life is headed.
  We must base our life on the foundation of God. The Spirit can and does lead us in loving ways. God is loving, kind, forgiving, and gentle. We are God's eyes, ears, hands, and feet in the world today. Our children learn unconditional love from us. They learn how to be loving (or not) by the way we interact with our husbands, our families, work associates, and our neighbors. When you think they are always watching and learning from everything we do, we realize the importance of the way we live. Setting a good, honest, loving example is vital.

Children do what we do, not what we say to do.

Julie recommends five strategies to overcome anger and abuse.

1) Base your life on the foundation of God. Have hope that God can change us.
2) Find a person you can be really honest with. Share your fears, angers, and ugly things with someone else. Get help, if needed.
3) Live lavishly – God wants us to be filled with grace and our joy to be lavish.
4) Make peace with your past. If you have anything in your past that has brought you pain or unresolved issues, deal with it.
5) Renew your mind in bite size pieces. Fill your mind with the truth. Get index cards and put on them. "Children are a reward from God." If you're Christian write, "I can do all things through Christ who strengthens me."

As Moms, we have got to *get real* with God, our self, and someone else.

The Power of Touch

Our children run to us with their "boo-boos" when they are hurt -- whether it's a headache, skinned knee, or bruised feelings. They come to us and want "Mommy, make it better." They want to be protected just like a baby bird waiting to be hatched. They need our touch and our physical support to be able to someday fly from the nest.

Moms have the healing power of touch. We can nurture and bring our children toward us for a little cuddle and TLC (Tender Loving Care). Touch can be healing. It can bring relief from pain, comfort, deep joy and contentment. We are loving, gentle, and tender. And as a Mom, we really can make most things better through a kiss, hug, or pat on the back.

Stay connected to your amazing healing power. You have the ability to creatively heal yourself and your family through loving touch.

How can you connect with loving touch?

- ❑ Set up a touching routine. Hug and kiss your children every morning, every night, and whenever they leave the house. (This obviously has to be altered for older kids especially when their friends are around.)

- ❑ Massage your children. You can start this even when they're in your belly.

- ❑ When disciplining, put your hand gently on your child's knee or shoulder to reinforce the message.

- ❑ Rub your child's head at night before bedtime or when they're sick. This soothes them and makes then relax and feel safe.

❑ Schedule a "Spa Time" in your own home. Include bubble bath, beautiful relaxing music, and candles. Give massages or manicures. This is really worth it when your kids get older and they're giving you massages back. Make this a special Mommy Care© bonding time.

❑ When waiting in lines or watching TV, rub their back and whisper something loving in their ear.

Loving touch fosters trust and creates an intimate bond between mother and child. Just as breast milk flows between a mother and child in infancy, touch is the healing energy that can flow throughout a lifetime. Because even when your children have flown out of the nest, they will always be your chickies.

The A/C Technique©

"Courage is doing what you are afraid to do.
There can be no courage unless you're scared."
Edward Rickenbacker

Just like air conditioning brings relief from the heat, the A/C technique© will bring relief from problems. Imagine if there were only three answers to solve every single problem. You might not really get three wishes from a genie, but you do have three ways to solve every problem.

The A/C Technique © Successful Coping Model

Avoid It   Alter It   Accept It

Avoiding Conflict and Problems

This includes removing yourself from the situation or figuring out how not to end up there in the first place! This may include:

- Saying "No"
- Walking away

- Delegating to someone else to handle the problem
- Letting go of your involvement

> One of the best ways to extinguish tantrums is to ignore them. T. Berry Brazelton, the renowned pediatrician and author, shared this essential rule: The more involved you are in trying to lessen the tantrum, the longer the tantrum will last. So pay no attention to your wailing kid, and try to go about your business so you don't reinforce his inappropriate behavior."

Altering Conflict

This implies removing the problem by changing something. Common techniques for altering are:

Compete – Approach where one person's concerns are at the other person's expense. Usually by overpowering the other through argument, threats, authority, or physical force. There is a clear winner and loser.

Collaborate – An approach where the people cooperate to find a mutually satisfactory solution. Both people are winners, neither is a loser.

Compromise – An approach that seeks partial satisfaction for both people through a middle-ground position requiring mutual sacrifice. Includes bargaining, exchanging concessions, and finding a fair combination of gains and losses for both people.

Accepting Conflict and Problems Exist

Really, problems are a natural part of living. This involves equipping oneself physically and emotionally for stress. Sometimes life hands us difficulties that we cannot fix, alter, or avoid. When this happens, we must accept the situation as it is.

My sister, Carlene, died from pancreatic cancer at the tender age of 39. During this difficult time my family prayed a lot. The amazing thing about prayer was it changed *us* so we could accept the situation and change our own attitude toward death. Acceptance does that. The problem doesn't change but our outlook of the problem changes.

Techniques to Acceptance

Build Your Own Resistance

- Proper diet, exercise, relaxation
- Mental attitude exercises
- Talk things over with girlfriends
- Build social support systems
- Spiritual Strength through prayer, faith, worship, or meditation
- Live in "day-tight" compartments -- take one day at a time. Yesterday is the past. Tomorrow is the future. Today is the present.

Change Your Perspective

- Vision a positive outcome
- Build your self-esteem through affirmations and uplifting self-talk
- Cultivate interests and hobbies that bring you joy
- Redefine the situation. Realize this too shall pass...

For me, I readily admit to being somewhat of a control-freak (at times) so acceptance has been the hardest problem-solving technique to master. The Serenity Prayer is still one of the best prayers for acceptance.

> *"God, grant me the serenity to*
> *Accept the things I cannot change,*
> *Courage to change the things I can,*
> *And the wisdom to know the difference."*

Pat Buckingham, a teacher and principal for the past 36 years has this story to tell about how children work out their differences in a peaceful way. Josh and Michael were in kindergarten. Michael took a pencil away from Josh and in the process jabbed Josh. First, Pat spoke to Michael and Josh individually.

Pat: Michael, tell me what happened?
Michael: The pencil touched Josh.
Pat: How did this happen?
Michael: I took the pencil away and it touched him.

They continued talking about the problem until Michael understood what he did wrong and how it made Josh feel.
Then Pat invited Josh to join them.

Pat: Josh, tell me what happened? (in a supportive, encouraging tone)
Josh: Michael stabbed me with the pencil. (See how there's two sides to every story.)
Pat: How did that make you feel?
Josh: (Looking at Michael) It hurt and I'm mad at you.

The kids talked about how Josh's feelings were hurt and how insulted he felt. It's so important that the children understand each other and can see things from the other person's perspective.

Pat: Michael, what can you do in the future so this doesn't happen again? What are you not going to do?
Michael: I can ask for a pencil or I can not grab it away
Pat: What can you do about the problem now?
Michael: I can apologize. (to Josh) I'm sorry. I didn't mean to hurt you.
Pat: (to Josh) What do you want to say to Michael?
Josh: It's okay, we can be friends again.
Pat: (to Michael) Why don't you just sit here and think about what happened.

Michael leaned over in the chair and fell asleep. He was totally exhausted.

At every age, it's important for children to talk out their differences and have consequences for their behavior. We have to be careful they are not humiliated. We need to change the behavior and separate the behavior from them as people. We have to let them know, "You're a great kid and you made a poor choice." We're helping them to internalize solving problems and how to make good choices. Often, children don't think first or anticipate consequences. As adults we need to model for them how they need to work things out.

I spoke to Sherley Kurtz, Principal of Driscoll Elementary School and she had these wise words. "The ultimate goal is for the child to learn independence. They need to internalize their behavior and make good choices. If parents are controlling -- the child only behaves as a result of his or her parents' presence.

Children need to work through the process of solving their own problems."

Sherley said most of the children who end up in her office get there by way of social issues – hitting, pushing, or stealing. She said these behaviors tend to be displayed most often during unstructured time (recess, lunch, walking to and from school or the bus stop) when an adult is not directly supervising them.

Her process for handling disputes:

1. Get the story clear about what really happened. She sees one person at a time so they can't influence each other. The stories are always different and she writes everything down. Then they work on fixing the story and finding out what really happened. Someone lies. "We've got to get the story straight so we know what happened. How did this happen? is a common question.

2. Once we're clear about who made the mistake, we focus on how it affects everyone. "Where is the problem?" or "How did you feel about it?" are typical questions

3. "What are we/you going to do to make it right? The child must come up with his or her own solutions.

4. Punishment fits the behavior. "The only reason for punishment is a change in behavior."

5. Follow up. She sees the child for a few days during recess and they continue to talk about what went on and what the child is thinking and doing differently.

Sherley says, "This process takes longer to work through, but it promotes long-term change among the child. It's so critical we teach the child responsibility and help them focus on solving their own problems before they get to middle school. Sometimes parents are very concerned about their kids' inappropriate behavior. We should be concerned because what we do now, determines how they act later on."

Can you imagine what the world would be like if all families and then all countries followed a peaceful approach to problem solving? Violence could be a distant memory. *We start change with one person at a time, then one family, one organization, one country, one world.*

Solving problems and dealing with conflict in a positive way is challenging. Sometimes unbearable. Mothering is tough at times. Go boldly. Be well prepared. Work in pairs and lean on others for support.

Wave the White Flag Proudly!

The Road to Victory - Surrender

He who would accomplish little must sacrifice little; he who would achieve much must sacrifice much."
- James Allen, Inspirational Author.

Coming to grips with who we are and where we're going is dependant upon an unusual companion called "surrender" - - as in "giving up." Not giving up our dreams but giving up how those dreams become a reality. Giving up our expectations of how something or someone "should" be.

Probably one of the most unexpected lessons I've learned as a Momager is about the power of sacrifice. If you came to my house, you may find a white hanky hanging from the kitchen light fixture, laying on the counter top, or even wrapped around my neck like a scarf. When I feel cranky or tired, I warn the family with a white hanky, which represents a white flag. The message is loud and clear. "Give up. Mom's in charge today and we need to be nice to her and do what she says." The kids know when they need to surrender.

The white flag also represents my need to surrender. I realize my efforts need to be united to God's in order to be successful. I surrender to God's authority and plan for my life. Just as we surrender to God, our children must surrender to our authority and leadership as parents.

Motherhood is filled with sacrifice and surrendering. When we become pregnant we surrender our bodies to create the victory of a precious child. We may surrender our careers in order to have enough time and a slower pace to raise healthy children. Both husband and wife have to surrender to each other over and over and over again to have the victory of a loving relationship. We may surrender our time to attend our children's activities, support their interests, and let them know they are important to us. We may surrender to the idea of having an immaculate house to gain the victory of a creative, fun home. We may need to surrender our ego in order to have the victory of truly understanding another person's viewpoint.

What have you had to sacrifice to be a Mom? What victories have you won as a result of surrendering?

1. _____

2. _____

3. _____

4. _____

5. _____

To lead others we must be willing to serve them and that includes surrendering. The surrender leads to ultimate victory. What would make you happy? Service. Leading. Loving. Sharing your gifts and talents with others. Having your own say in your own unique way.

To conclude this chapter, I leave you with the words of syndicated radio show host, Paul Harvey.

We tried so hard to make things better for our kids that we made them worse.

For my grandchildren, I'd like better.

I'd really like for them to know about hand me down clothes and homemade ice cream and leftover meat loaf sandwiches. I really would.

I hope you learn humility by being humiliated, and that you learn honesty by being cheated.

I hope you learn to make your own bed and mow the lawn and wash the car.

And I really hope nobody gives you a brand new car when you are sixteen.

It will be good if at least one time you can see puppies born and your old dog put to sleep.

I hope you get a black eye fighting for something you believe in.

I hope you have to share a bedroom with your younger brother/sister. And it's all right if you have to draw a line down the middle of the room, but when he wants to crawl under the covers with you because he's scared, I hope you let him.

When you want to see a movie and your little brother/sister wants to tag along, I hope you'll let him/her.

I hope you have to walk uphill to school with your friends and that you live in a town where you can do it safely.

On rainy days when you have to catch a ride, I hope you don't ask your driver to drop you two blocks away so you won't be seen riding with someone as uncool as your Mom.

If you want a slingshot, I hope your Dad teaches you how to make one instead of buying one.

I hope you learn to dig in the dirt and read books.

When you learn to use computers, I hope you also learn to add and subtract in your head.

I hope you get teased by your friends when you have your first crush on a boy\girl, and when you talk back to your mother that you learn what ivory soap tastes like.

May you skin your knee climbing a mountain, burn your hand on a stove and stick your tongue on a frozen flagpole.

I don't care if you try a beer once, but I hope you don't like it. And if a friend offers you dope or a joint, I hope you realize he/she is not your friend.

I sure hope you make time to sit on a porch with your Grandma/Grandpa and go fishing with your Uncle.

May you feel sorrow at a funeral and joy during the holidays.

I hope your mother punishes you when you throw a baseball through your neighbor's window and that she hugs you and kisses you at Hanukkah/Christmas time when you give her a plaster mold of your hand.

These things I wish for you - tough times and disappointment, hard work and happiness. To me, it's the only way to appreciate life.

Chapter 9

Y - Because You are Valuable and The World Needs Your Unique Contribution

"My mother was the most beautiful woman I ever saw.
All I am I owe to my mother. I attribute all my success in life to the moral,
intellectual and physical education I received from her."
-George Washington

Momagers Rule!

Momagers are powerful and influential leaders. Our very role as Moms is to have authority and influence with the next generation of leaders. We have the power to teach our children right from wrong. We have the power to make rules and enforce what's best for our family. We are responsible for our children. We have the privilege of being in charge. We have the power to reach our fullest potential and have a meaningful life. We have the power to leave a loving and lasting legacy.

The trouble is, many mothers don't recognize their role as leaders. Some mothers let other people raise their kids and relinquish their power. When we're separated from our kids' daily events and responsibilities, we lose our authority and power. I hope this book will help change that. Now I don't want you to feel badly if you work outside the home. I truly believe each woman has to make that decision herself. It's an issue of balancing your time, energy, and resources to do what's best for you and your family.

My sincerest hope is we will regain our dignity and influence as mothers. The world needs our valuable contributions and the world begins with our family, our children. Let me share a story that Mother Theresa told in the book *Words to Love By.*

"I once picked up a child of six or seven in the street and took her to Shishu Bhavin (a children's home) and gave her a bath, some clothes and some nice food. That evening, the child ran away. We took the child in a second and a third time, and she ran away. After the third time I sent a sister to follow her. The sister found the child sitting with her mother and sister under a tree. There was a little dish there and the mother was cooking food she had picked up from the streets. They were cooking there, they were eating there, they were sleeping there. It was their home. And then we understood why the child ran away. The mother just loved that child. And the child loved the mother. They were so beautiful to each other. The child said "bari jabo" -- it was her home. Her mother was her home."

Generational Leadership©

Our role as Moms is to unconditionally love our children so they will be secure in that love for a lifetime. The leadership I'm talking about is *'Generational Leadership©*. The values, love, and dignity we instill in our children will span -- not only with the next generation -- but many generations to come. I am forever grateful to my Mom and Grandma for believing in my uniqueness and providing a foundation in faith. Their words of encouragements still echo in my mind at important times. "You can do it." "You will do good things." These words, and the confidence they instill stick for a lifetime.

Unfortunately, our society and companies are focused on short-term results. This philosophy doesn't transfer to home life. American culture doesn't recognize mother's authority either. Our society values independence and financial power over community spirit and family obligations. Surely there's room to value all these things.

Yes, we get lip-service on Mother's Day. But think about it. When was the last time you got a call from a reporter asking for a quote on family issues? Are you considered an expert on children and community building? Why do we continue to rely on professional psychological "experts?"

The latest book I've seen about "being a mom for the first time" is written by a man! What is up with *that*? We have the knowledge, skills, and abilities. Why don't more women have a voice to express what we are experiencing? Women have been raising kids for thousands of years. Moms are the experts at child development.

Trust Your Instincts

"Often intuition will direct you.
If it feels right, it's probably right."
-- Oprah Winfrey

Momagers have strong instincts regarding their children and what's best for their families. As women, we have deep emotions that tell us when something is right and when something is wrong. We can tap into our amazing well of intuition and follow through on what is best.

Let's take the example of dealing with sick children. Kids don't come with a set of instructions and when they're small, we don't always know when they're sick enough to go to the doctor or when we're being overprotective. Usually your "gut" will lead you in the right direction.

When my youngest son, Steven was just three months old he developed a cough. For a few days I said to my husband, "Do you think we should take him to do the doctor?" I had this niggling feeling that something was wrong. "Oh no, it's probably just a cold and cough." Bob kept saying. He wanted to wait the usual 7-10 days for the cold to pass. By the fourth day I felt so strongly about his condition that I brought him to the doctor.

Steven had pneumonia! I was furious. Why didn't I trust my instincts? After that incident I told Bob that I would always trust my instincts and he had to respect that sometimes there won't be logical reasons for me to make decisions about our family. He agreed and now I'm much happier with using my gift of intuition. Sometimes other people will put logic into their decision making, and that may be fine for them. After you've thought through a situation, then follow your gut.

As Momagers, we have to trust our instincts and recognize the power they contain. Trust your instincts and don't let anyone talk you out of them. They are too valuable to reason away.

Societies Support (or lack thereof) for Moms

What types of societal support systems do we have for moms? What types of continuing education are offered? How much do you get paid for being a mom? What legislative influence do mom's have for issues affecting our children and us?

European cultures are light years ahead of us in family issues. They have longer paid maternity leave benefits, get paid to be "stay-at-home parents," and actually have influence within the government. I gave birth to our first child in England, and get this, I was paid to be a "mom." That's right! Once a month I received my check in the mail from the government. Granted, it wasn't much, but it was enough to make me feel appreciated and recognized. The point is they valued the contribution mothers were making and were willing to invest in us. A salary is paid to all mothers in a number of countries including Britain and France.

When I lived in England I was going through the check-out line and I noticed there weren't any candy bars. "Why don't you have candy here? I asked the cashier. "Oh, we used to. Mothers got sick of listening to their kids moaning for candy so they lobbied and got the candy removed." I stood there speechless.

Do mothers in this country have that much leveraging power? How many other policies affect us and go unchallenged? What can the government, the media, stores, schools, banks, and hospitals do to support Moms more? We have a lot of work to change policies that are not child friendly or family friendly.

The way I see it, we have some agenda items that need to be addressed.

➤ Why don't we have more paid maternity leave?
➤ Why isn't more money being invested in our children through the public schools?
➤ Why don't Momagers get paid to care for children? Wouldn't it be great to get a realistic child allowance that is paid to all primary caregivers?
➤ Why don't all Americans have health-care coverage?
➤ Why don't we have high-quality, affordable or free, pre-schools for kids?

> ➢ Why don't we have more support for new and all mothers?
> ➢ Why can't every single parent get education on parenting and childhood development?
> ➢ Why do we have a culture that separates stay-at-home from working moms?
> ➢ Who is going to champion that all children have a safe society to play in?
> ➢ Why doesn't every community in America have a community center that supports families with activities, parenting education, and pediatric clinics?

Maybe we need to form a Momager group to represent Moms issues. How about a Mom PAC-Political Action Committee? I could go on and on, but you get the point. Do you have a list of injustices we can work on? As moms, we've lost our way. *The good news is we can find it -- by valuing and empowering each other.*

We need to change our attitude about what mothers do and give all mothers the respect they deserve. We must value our mothering time and see it as the leadership development opportunity it is. We must value our contribution to our families and society. Let's stand up and take some credit for our profession. Let our voice be heard and let it ring through all the institutions that affect us.

"What do you do all day?"

Every day the question comes. "What did you do today?" you ask your children. "Not much," they reply. I've changed the question to, "Tell me about something good that happened today." They have to come up with something.

Your husband asks you the same question. You list your activities. "I fed the kids, cleaned the house, volunteered at school, helped them with homework, drove them to practice . . ." As you're relaying the information, do you truly believe you are doing the most important job in the world? If so, it will come across in everything you do. If not, the doubt will creep into your very being and your relationships. Oh, and by the way, if you hear, "Is that all?" you have full permission to "let 'em have it!" Momagers do not accept minimizing of our career!

Before you "report" on your day, give it the status and dignity it truly deserves. We may doubt how truly valuable we are. Our children know better. Ask any child who doesn't have a mom around and they'll tell you.

Steve Huber is the father of three boys and he lost his wife to cancer. He became the full-time homemaker. "I'm amazed at the volume of work that goes into being a homemaker -- the vacuuming, laundering, food shopping, and endless picking up of toys. I am the boys' arbitrator for sibling disputes, their schedule coordinator, their personal homework assistant, and their chef.

"I used to see at-home moms and think to myself, 'What do you do all day?' Now I know: It's a demanding job that makes going out to work every day look like a breeze. I've often heard people say, 'I wish I'd spent less time at work because I missed seeing my kids.' I hope to resume my career when the boys are older, and when I do, I won't have any such regrets. Though I used to hear about the boys' milestones from Laura, I now get to experience them all firsthand. Every once in a while, one of the kids will say to me, 'I wish Mommy was here.' I do too."

How many children are thinking, "I wish Mommy was here," when their mothers are alive? You have a choice to be there or not. Without us, our children feel an irreplaceable void that no one else can fill.

Momagers are Queens

I wish every mother would think of herself as a queen of the home. My husband calls me "Queen Christine" sometimes and I just love it. As a matter of fact, he did this before we even got married. Of course, that makes him "King Bob." At our wedding reception we each wore crowns. Let me suggest you buy or make a crown. What would be on it? Diamonds, rubies, emeralds, gold? Or would you rather have pictures of your husband and kids? How about both? Whatever you choose to put on your crown is a reflection of you. How much are you worth? How much do you value yourself?

Mirror, Mirror on the Wall,
Who's the Fairest of them All?

You!

To value yourself more you can wear your crown, look in the mirror and tell yourself all the things you're proud of. Maybe you spoke in a kind way to your kids today. (Which can be extremely challenging some days). Maybe you exercised. Maybe you volunteered at school. Maybe you started or finished a project. Maybe you made a healthy dinner and your family ate together. Whatever you do, take the time to tell yourself how truly precious you are. Rather than giving you a big head, this will give you appreciation and confidence. As women, we need to recognize our contribution -- no matter what it is.

And how about having our kids honor us? Once in a while my husband will lead the kids in a chant, "We honor Mommy." "Thank you for working so hard for us, Mommy." They get down on their knees and fan their hands up and down. It's so much fun and it sure does make me feel appreciated.

My daughter Tina Rose loves to do cheers and once in a while she'll do a cheer for me. "Two, Four, Six, Eight, Who do we appreciate? Mommy, Mommy, Yea!" I think being on a throne and being honored is our rightful place as Momagers, don't you?

Why the World Needs Momagers to be Strong Leaders

There is no doubt that children in America are in trouble.

- Over one million children a year are victims of child abuse and neglect. (Most experts agree the number is actually much higher, because many abuse cases are never reported.)
- More than a 200% increase in the teenage suicide rate since 1960.
- 560 percent increase in violent crime among children since 1960.
- Childhood depression is at an all time high

- The number one form of abuse in our country is neglect: 46 percent of our kids are emotionally and psychologically neglected. Physical and sexual child abuses are increasing.
- One in three kids live in a home without enough nurturing and support.
- A tripling of the percentage of children living in single-parent homes since 1960. Kids in single-parent homes have a lower measure of academic achievement, higher level of stress, depression, aggression, anxiety, more sexual experiences and substance abuse problems.
- 419 percent increase in illegitimate births since 1960.
- Research has shown that 73 percent of boys and 78 percent of girls between the ages of 12 and19 watch MTV for more than six hours a week. It is clear that MTV has a deep and powerful saturation of youth culture and, in fact, is a defining factor of youth culture sexual values, not a reflection of them. MTV's half time show at Super Bowl '04 showed the world its agenda to redefine sexuality among today's youth into behavior that is destructive. Eighty-nine *million* people worldwide witnessed blatant sexuality and the deliberate exploitation of women.
- Neglecting an infant can affect brain development and all future relationships. Feelings of abandonment stay for a lifetime.
- Without trust, children become withdrawn, antisocial, insecure and have trouble with relationships.

Ryan Dobson, who teaches teenagers about absolute truth, right and wrong, said the following on a Focus on the Family radio interview:

"Teenagers nowadays are hurting. They are angry and rebellious because they want to be loved. Kids are looking for boundaries. Looking for the right way to go. Parents can't know everything but they do know how to love. Parenting is a tough job. Families are just too busy. Their role is to teach unconditional love. Kids want this love."

Who is going to champion for our children and our influence as parents? Is the government, media, or business going to spearhead changes for our children? They will. Only after we have stood up and stated our concerns and needs.

The Momager Movement

"All that is important is this one moment in movement.
Make the moment vital and worth living.
Do not let it slip away unnoticed and unused."
-Martha Graham, Dancer

Momagers must lead the way each and every day. We start by valuing ourselves and our families. Then we let our voices be heard with government, schools, work places, community groups and hospitals. If there's a policy you want to see enacted, call, write, or e-mail your representative and ask them, "What are you going to do about paid maternity leave, or a realistic tax break for an at-home parent?"

If there's something happening that you don't think is in the best interest of your family, express your opinions and feelings. We must speak up more. We must become more political. (And this is coming from a person who hasn't had confidence in politicians.) It's our vehicle for legislative power, ladies. Momagers must be the voice for our children and families.

The Power of Birth and Creation

Let's start right at the beginning and see the preciousness of conception. At that very moment the Creator sees you as worthy enough to be a co-creator of human life. Let that sink in for a moment. You were chosen to create and re-create another human being. This honor brings with it an awesome responsibility.

Giving birth contains tremendous power and it contains the power of love. Our love is multiplied in another living, breathing, miraculous human life. Mothers lay down their lives, their figures, and their sleep, for their children.

As we have seen in the last 30 years, not everyone is so lucky. Even with all our scientific breakthroughs some women simply cannot have children. Why is that? Has science just not developed enough or is there a divine plan for each child?

After birth, while breast-feeding, you sustain the baby in its crucial first year. The mother, alone, has the best nutrients and nurturing time to sustain the baby. Your body and mind have been crafted for creation and to give the best of yourself to your family.

Your True Value is in Your Loving Legacy

As Momagers, we have to get rid of all the "media baggage" about our worth. How valuable you are isn't determined by the amount of money you have in your bank account. My father says, "You can't attach a U-haul to the hearse in your funeral procession." It's true. All the money and possessions you have will stay right here on earth. Your value isn't determined by how beautiful or young you are. Your value isn't even based on how much you do.

Like the most precious diamond, your value lies in the facets of love you radiate. Your hallmark will be how much love you share with others. Who you are and how much love you pour into everything you do determines how valuable you are. The love you leave in each person and especially your family will bring you crowning glory.

What Do Momagers Teach and Learn?

"The Mother's Heart is the Child's Schoolroom."
-Henry Ward Beecher

As a Momager, your life is a school filled with memorable – and not so memorable -- moments. Sometimes you are a teacher and other times you're a student. Lessons can be taught and learned in unlikely places and faces.

Your children teach you how to handle enormous responsibility -- how to laugh and cry and live in the moment. They teach you how important it is to look into the future, yet live for today. Play. Enjoy all your senses. Live lavishly. Your children teach you how to live fully and remind you that now is the only moment you have.

Your children teach you how to lead and find meaning outside of yourself. They teach you how to handle overwhelming emotions. As a mom, you will forever wear your heart and emotions outside, not inside your body. You become more vulnerable. Your children teach you how connected you are to other people and to the environment. After all, the next generation needs to live on the earth.

Children teach us patience and perseverance. (It takes a long time to see them develop into adults.) In our short-term society, our children teach us the importance of waiting and waiting and waiting. Raising kids is *at least* an 18-year project. Notice the most important words in the last sentence were – at least. You never stop being a mom. You never stop thinking about your kids and then your grandkids. Being a Momager is a role that is yours for your entire life.

Children teach us how to give birth and create and re-create. Feel the power you contain to create and sustain another human being. During pregnancy, we wait nine months for our children to come into the world. Then we devote a lifetime to teaching them to sustain their own life. We spend every single day of our life connected to them emotionally and spiritually so they can sustain their life without us being physically present. Children teach us how to have true happiness by finding ourselves, through giving to another.

Like a mother bird that lets her baby birds try their wings and fly, we must give our children strong wings so they can soar. We can teach them how to be accountable and have strong character. We can teach them, and then we can let them go. The circle of life will continue.

As teachers, we show them how to be good and responsible people. There are so many firsts and lasts that we teach. Every first for them is a last for the way things were before. And with each first we let go.

The First Time They:	The Last Time:
Say a word	We have quiet
Take a step	We stay still
Use the potty	We change a diaper
Are sick	We care about our own health first
Say "no"	We say "yes" to everything.
Ride a bike	We hold onto the seat

Go to school	We teach them everything
Get into a fight	We think they're angels
Read	We are the "exclusive" story reader
Talk on the phone	We have unlimited use of the phone
Take the car out	We have control over where they go
Are rejected	They let someone else rule their emotions
Make a basket, goal, or hit	They wonder if they can do it
Go on a date	They tell us everything
Break up	We say everyone loves them
Get a job	They are responsible only to their family
Have a child	You're the only mother. Congrats -- now you're a grandma!

And so the cycle of life contains the passage of time, lessons taught and lessons learned. Everyone says, "They grow up so fast." Some days seem to fly by at lightning speed, other days are way too slow.

As a Momager, your children need you to teach them all about life and love. So, here are the Top Ten (BIG) Topics you need to teach them.

How To:

- Unconditionally Love
- Trust
- Learn
- Work hard
- Support themselves and others financially
- Be a good person who does the right things
- Be in healthy relationships
- Make a contribution
- Use their skills and talents
- Have fun!

Our time of influence will indeed pass away too quickly. We only have a certain amount of time to teach them how to be confident, responsible, happy people. Use your time wisely or it will be gone before you know it.

Are You Wasting Away or

Doing 'The Most Important Thing?"

I've heard women say, "How could you stay at home with your kids and 'waste' all your education?" I truly don't believe that one second is EVER wasted on family. What you are, is precisely what your family needs. You're not wasting your time or talents by investing energy and love in your family. You are fulfilling your most important role.

I'll be honest, when my children were young, at first, I longed to work outside the home. I missed my full-time career. I missed not having a coffee break or a lunch break or any break for that matter. I missed not talking to people around the water cooler. I missed not using my brain to its fullest capacity, let alone being able to carry on an adult conversation. I missed not getting recognition and awards for my performance. I remember thinking, "Am I wasting away?" "Who is this woman in the mirror with crazy hair and baggy clothes and a mono-syllable vocabulary?" Certainly it wasn't me. Then I realized, it *was* me -- *for a time.*

Was I wasting away? No. I changed and became a new person -- a new creation. We do this over and over again in our lives. With every change in lifestyle there is a time of letting go and adjustment. Was it worth it? You bet! This book is a product of that feeling of lost identity -- that was found. May you strengthen in your Momager identity.

No one role is who we are in our entirety so it's important to go with the flow and be multi-dimensional. Do what you can, when you can, to make a meaningful contribution. Momaging should be seen as an asset and an incredible leadership development time.

Most of all, love yourself. Be kind, gentle, patient, and forgiving with yourself and then your love will overflow to others. Love yourself so much so you can be happy and you can be YOU.

What do you do? Do you work?

I've been asked this question so often that I've lost count. Instead of watching the disdainful look of single women or bored men, I now have an exciting, updated, fun, career. You do too. You have a new identity and a new title to put on your resume. When employers or people at cocktail parties ask you, "What do you do?" answer, "I'm a MOMAGER," and note their interested reaction. "Did you say manager?" "I'm a MOMAGER of the Martinello (fill in your family name) Enterprise."

You'll be armed and ready with some innovative ideas and stories to share about your leadership role. Give 'em an earful. Tell them how you apply VICTORY© to your life. Tell them how you vision, influentially communicate, constantly deal with change, build a strong team, organize and balance, resolve conflicts and problem solve. Let them know that you're a great leader and how valuable you truly are!

Momagers' work is not invisible or "time off." We are working and we are hardworking. It's about time we proclaim it to the world and change our culture's view of mothers. Let's celebrate Motherhood! Traditionally, women have been defined by what we are to other people -- mother, daughter, sister, wife. This has certainly changed. Today, women are valued, not only for our relationships, but also for our merit. There's practically no limit to what we can be, do, and achieve.

Women have had to overcome many challenges throughout history. We've spent so much time focused on success and independence that now our greatest challenges lie in loving, balancing, and leaving a legacy.

It is time to reclaim our power.
It is time to reclaim our crowns.
It is time to reclaim our families.
It is time to reclaim our communities,
and make a better, more humane world.

What contribution will you make?

What legacy will you leave?

Never limit the power you have.

I will be cheering for you and encouraging you.

Walk on to VICTORY©.

To Realize

To realize
The value of a mother,
Ask someone
Who doesn't have one.
To realize
The value of ten years,
Ask a newly
Divorced couple.
To realize
The value of four years,
Ask a graduate.
To realize
The value of one year,
Look at how much a child grows.
To realize
The value of nine months,
Ask a mother who gave birth to a stillborn.
To realize
The value of one month,
Ask a mother who has
Given birth to a premature baby.
To realize
The value of one hour,
Ask the lovers who are waiting to meet.
To realize
The value of one-second,
Ask a person
Who has survived an accident.
To realize
The value of one millisecond,
Ask the person who has
Won a silver medal in the Olympics.
To realize the value of a friend,

Lose one.
Time waits for no one.
Treasure every moment you have.
You will treasure it even more when
you can share it with someone special.
Author Unknown

About The Author

Christine Martinello, President of Training Solutions International since 1993, is a recognized authority on leadership, teambuilding, and communications. She presents keynote speeches and seminars both nationally and internationally.

She is a highly motivating speaker with corporate and non-profit clients including Merrill Lynch, Iams Corp, Girl Scouts of America and the US Dept. of Energy among others.

Christine is a media-featured speaker and appeared on the European Business News with more than 40 million viewers, and WONE Radio.

She has been married to Bob for 11 years and is a Momager of three school-aged children. She is a community leader, served on the board of Caring Families and Ministry of Mothers Sharing M.O.M.S.'s, and is the founder of Cheltenham Women's Group. She resides in Dayton, OH.

❑ To book Christine Martinello for a speaking engagement, please contact:
Training Solutions Int'l
P. O. Box 752295
Dayton, OH
937. 428.7951

❑ To order your free Empowering Leaders e-newsletter visit www.christinemartinello.com

For more information visit **www.christinemartinello.com**

❑ Yes! **Please send me extra copies of** *The Momager Guide; Empowering Moms to Leave A Loving Legacy for my family/friends!*

The Momager Guide _____ **copies X $ ($14.99 soft cover**
                                        $24.99 hard cover) = $_____

Add 10% shipping & handling (4.50 minimum) $_____

Total (U.S. Dollars only) $_____

Name _____ Title _____
Organization _____ Phone_____
Shipping Address _____ Fax_____
City _____ State_____ Zip _____
e-mail address _____
❑   Check enclosed (Payable to Training Solutions Intl)

CPSIA information can be obtained at www.ICGtesting.com
Printed in the USA
LVOW072310181111

255659LV00002B/6/A